I0380365

ALMOST TO Heaven

Almost to Heaven

JEAN NIELSEN

ISBN Softcover 978-1-950596-90-4

Printed in the United States of America.

To order additional copies of this book, contact:
Bookwhip
1-855-339-3589
www.bookwhip.com

Table of Contents

Special Acknowledgements

To God, To Whom I owe my entire being— heart, body and soul— I'm so grateful for another chance, and will strive to serve You as You Will, not mine, in full Communion of the Church.

To my family, husband, Rod, daughters, Louise and Rose, my son-in-law, Bruce, and family friend, Ashley, three granddaughters. Lola, Emily, and Peggy all who graciously stood by me, and prayed through all of this.

To Mom and Dad, sisters, aunts, uncles, and cousins who prayed, and asked others' to pray for me, too.

To the New Ulm Medical Center, NUMC thank you for your great care and expertise.

To Dr. Jeff Rayl-thank you for your care and expertise, and choosing to work with the NUMC.

To Kitty-New Ulm Medical Center's Communication and Marketing Specialist-thank you for recognizing my letter to the editor. The book was written partly, because of your work in noticing my Letter to the Editor.

To Sara-thank you for your extra effort in arranging my visit with Dr. Rayl.

To Abbott Northwestern Hospital, thank you for your expertise and care, especially for acknowledging the work of the New Ulm

Medical Center-that comment was a key component for me in writing my book.

To Dr. Tim Henry-thank you for your care, time and tenacious spirit working with me. I was Blessed to have the top cardiologist who "happened" to be on call that morning at Abbott at the time I needed one the most. Thank you for your personal touch when you called to explain Stem Cell Research to me. I would never have taken the time to research what Stem Cell Research was on my own.

ToNorth Memorial Air/Ambulance- thank you for your quickness, care, donation, and calmness.

To St. Mary's parishioners and priest, your prayers are heard.

To the New Ulm Public Library, thank you to the staff forpatiently working with me on all this computer technology!

To my friends Marge and Marion, who spent countless hours assisting with editing, reading, and who's encouragement and wisdom brought my book to it's fruition, thank you is not enough!

To neighbors, thank you for all your help and prayers.

To employers, the assisted living facility, Orchard Hills, Habilitative Services, Inc., New Ulm public and parochial schools, Sleepy Eye Migrant school, and all Early Childhood programs, thank you for helping me renew my licenses to teach and work with the children you serve.

To Adam Towles, owner ForeSee Studios, New Ulm, Mnnesota. Thank you for your time and care assisting with copying of my book.

To New Ulm, Minnesota, a quiet city 90 miles southwest of the Twin Cities for your thoughtfulness, prayers and support during my recovery.

To the Green Bay Packers, thanks for the values you place on your team!

To friends from North Dakota, Fosston, Wisconsin, Iowa, and other numerous states and countries too countless to name. Thank you for your prayers, even if you didn't know who I am.

To Aunt Tub, who placed my name on her order's prayer chain, where 200 nuns prayed for me.

May only good come out of my book!

To ALL of you, know that ALL I DO AND SAY WILL BE DONE IN THE FULLNESS OF GOD'S GRACE TO GLORIFY HIS NAME!

Thank you.

Love and Sincerely in Christ,

Jean Nielsen

CHAPTER 1:

THE TRIP

A heart attack? Oh, c'mon! No! I was a 52-year-old female, and in good health. I weighed 115 lbs., and I was 5'2" tall. My blood pressure readings always registered in the lower-100s-lower-60s. My cholesterol levels always stayed within normal limits! Yet, I was sweating and after ten minutes of sweating, shortness of breath came. I assumed the sweating and shortness of breath were menopause issues or the flu. I'm too young for a heart attack.

The date was August 26, 2013. I was scheduled for the 10:00 p.m. to 6:00 a.m. shift. I brushed off the sweating and shortness of breath symptoms as nerves since I had started a new position as a Resident-Care Provider (RCP) at an assisted living facility. This position was in addition to another full-time position I had with Habilitative Services, Inc. (HSI) as a Team Lead Assist (TLA). I knew those symptoms could be the signs of a heart attack, but this was my first shift alone after training at a new place of employment; I attributed the symptoms I had to nerves.

As the symptoms continued, I called the Lead Care Provider (LCP) to cover my shift. Thankfully, I had known the LCP for the 13 years I had worked with her through HSI. I figured she would know I wasn't faking the illness when I called her to relieve me on my first shift off training. Many others left after a day in that position.

I had called my husband, Rod continuously for a ride home, since I felt so light-headed. I didn't want to risk driving myself. However, I hadn't had any luck reaching him. The only other means of public transportation in New Ulm that the city offered, was the taxi. At that time, the taxi was closed for business, because it was a Sunday night.

As a last resort, I had the ambulance to call for a ride home. But how? How could I justify calling 911 simply for a ride home, let alone the expense!

Around 12:50 a.m., my heart started racing, more like fluttering. The fluttering reminded me of when I was a little girl, and learned how to ride a bike. Once I learned, the cool thing to do was attach a playing card to your spokes with a clothespin. Then, when I peddled, the card would make a neat fluttering sound.

I knew that my heart fluttering was a very different feeling, not normal. After seconds, the fluttering stopped. I thought the fluttering was my imagination, since it was so quick. But, the feeling was so strong, I figured the fluttering couldn't be my imagination.

I reasoned if I called 911, the worst case scenario was the New Ulm Medical Center, (NUMC), will run a couple of tests, give me a couple pills, call whatever I had the flu or something, and then send me home; and that's what they want to do with a case anyway, send you home. I never dreamed I called them because I needed to have transportation to Abbott in the Twin Cities.

Finally, because I didn't have any other choice, I decided to call 911. I looked at the clock, and the time was 1:00 a.m. I called 911, told the operator what the emergency was, location, and where I was at the assisted living facility, which was right at the front door. Being at the front door was a miracle, as I had already been throughout the building, checked on residents, and finished all major tasks.

The operator dispatched the ambulance, which arrived in five minutes! When they came, I looked at the clock, and the time was literally 1:05 a.m. The police were right behind them. It is typical that the police accompany 911 calls in New Ulm, Minnesota, in case additional help was needed. This is how the community works together.

I cringed a bit as the ambulance and police arrived. I opened the front door for them. As the team came in with the gurney, oxygen tank, blood pressure cup, and other equipment they might need, I thought, geez, here they are bringing all of these things in for someone who only has the flu. I felt bad they were doing all this extra work for me, when basically I only called them for a ride home. I also thought, the ER doctors at the Medical Center would think of my arrival as the most ridiculous case they ever had as a reason for an emergency: I needed a ride home.

I couldn't tell who these people were, I could only hear their voices. There were three team members. One of the team members asked; "Jean, can you help us lift you up on the gurney?" I shook my head yes, and assisted with positioning myself on the gurney.

Another team member said, "Jean, I'm going to put three baby aspirins under your tongue. They should dissolve, okay". I shook my head acknowledging that fact.

One team member started putting the blood pressure cup around my right arm. He asked, "Jean, do you smoke?" I shook my head no. He asked, "Were you out in the heat today for a long time?" The day was excruciatingly hot, over 95 degrees in the shade, which was why he asked if I was in the heat for a long time. I shook my head no again, as I worked at HSI before coming here, so had been in an air-conditioned house all day. Those were all the questions I remembered that they asked.

At that point, the LCP came. That was a relief for me, because I knew she would take care of the residents. The LCP said, "Jeannie, do you want me to call Rod?" The staff called me Jeannie at the assisted living facility, because there were two of us with the name Jean. Once I was offered the position, the director asked, "Would it be okay to call me Jeannie, since we have two staff with the same name, and you came second." A couple others have called me Jeannie, and I didn't mind. I said, "Sure."

I shook my head yes to the LCP, and thought maybe she'll have better luck reaching him. The LCP left for the office, I assumed to call Rod.

Next, the team strapped me on the gurney, rolled me out of the building, lifted me into the ambulance, and then closed the door. I thought well, these guys will take me to the New Ulm Medical Center. I felt reassured here, because I knew from previous experience that I would be in good hands at the NUMC. I told myself again, the doctors will run a couple of tests, determine that I only had the flu; they'd prescribe some medications, and send me home.

I remembered the ambulance turning around in the parking lot at the assisted living facility, and driving up to a set of stoplights on one of New Ulm' main highways. After that, I blacked out until at some point and time, I awoke at the ER.

Once in the ER on that frightful morning, doctors and nurses worked on me, although I don't know what really happened. Not only was I semi-conscious, but I couldn't see who was doing what; I heard voices once in a while. That was all. At some point, an ER doctor made a call to Abbott.

I remembered a nurse asking, "Jean, do you drink any morealcohol than your family knows about?" I shook my head no, and thought that was an odd question. Mostly, I shook my head no because, frankly, I wasn't sure what my family had told them! I remembered being relieved that they had finally managed to contact Rod, although I didn't know how.

Other conversations were going on. At some point, a nurse told me that I had a catheter. I wondered why, since I planned to go home. I certainly didn't need a catheter. C'mon! I only had the flu!

Meanwhile, someone called for a helicopter.

At one point, I heard our oldest daughter, Louise. She said, "Mom, you can't go home with this, okay?" Then, I don't remember what happened for a while.

A few minutes later, other people emerged. I remembered a nurse from the helicopter came into the room and told me, "Jean, John has been doing this for more than 20 years, so you're in good hands."

I thought that was a funny comment because I was already in good hands. I was in New Ulm. I tried to tell this person that, but nothing came out. I figured my family must have told them I was afraid of flying, which I am.

My next memory was of my being lifted into the helicopter. I don't remember going from my hospital room to the helicopter or even where my family was at this time. As they lifted me into the helicopter, my husband tried to reassure me that I was on my way to the best heart hospital in the world.

I wondered, *Why? Why am I being transported to the best heart hospital in the world? Sure, I'm sweating, have shortness of breath, and felt nauseated. Aren't those symptoms menopausal or the flu? I've experienced them several times before and didn't need care like this!*

Then I thought, Maybe this is what they do, send patients to Abbott by air, when someone calls them only for a ride home-as a form of punishment. After I thought that, I said, to myself, No, that would be a really ridiculous form of punishment, and a total waste of time and money, especially if someone else needed an ambulance; to punish someone for needing a ride home when they were sick.

My feet were next to the pilot's head, and my head was inches from the other nurse. The ceiling of the helicopter felt like it was right on top of me. I couldn't move if I wanted to. I thought, *Boy! There's not much room in these things.*

I tried to tell them that this attention was all very nice, but I didn't need it, as I lived only a couple of blocks away. I also wondered where the heck they were going to land the helicopter at our house as our lot was certainly too small for a helicopter to land. Oops! Too late! I couldn't manage to say the words. They shut the door, and we lifted. I thought, *Wow, that was quick! Oh well… I don't have a choice now! I guess I'm going home by helicopter?*

I couldn't see the crew's faces, only heard them. Then the nurse told me, "Jean, we're going to take you to Abbott." As soon as they told me I was going to Abbott, I thought, *Abbott? This isn't going to be good.*

Almost immediately after that thought, the nurse said, "Jean, I'm going to shock you now."

I said, "No! I'm scared."

He didn't say anything. He shocked me. That felt like I was running into an electric fence, only stronger. The shock didn't hurt. My body jumped with the shock, and then I was out until we arrived in Minneapolis.

I awoke when the helicopter descended into Minneapolis, although in the report, it stated I was alert and teary-eyed during the entire flight. I opened my eyes and saw the pretty lights from the city. Yes, I knew the lights were from the city. I saw the amber colors. As I looked at them, I thought, *Gee, those lights are actually kind of pretty from up here. This flying business isn't so bad!* The helicopter started descending, and I specifically felt it drop 3 times.

The emergency personnel somehow knew I was alert.

After the first drop, the nurse said, "Jean, I see you have hearing aids."

I shook my head yes.

He said, "I'm going to take them out now. Can you hear without them?"

I felt the second drop. I put two fingers together that resembled the idea of being able to hear a little bit, because I couldn't speak by now. I couldn't feel him taking them out, but I heard them klunk into the cup as he dropped them.

Then I felt the third drop. I waited for the nurse to say more, but he didn't. I thought, *Well, I guess whatever's going to happen is going to happen now, and I hope I did some good!* I don't know if I had a premonition or an inkling of what might lay ahead, but that was my last earthly memory for a while.

I realized quickly how fragile life was, how mortal I was, and how much I had taken my life for granted. I closed my eyes, and had the most amazing, but scariest experience of my life: A HEART-TO-HEART VISIT WITH GOD!

Chapter 2:

Where Am I?

I didn't have a grand entrance into that area, wherever I was. But suddenly, there I was. I stood up from a position as if I were doing a toe touch as a marionette. The area itself was dark and gray all around me, much like I might see on a foggy, dreary morning or on a snowy TV, but darker in a way.

As I stood up, I saw a dark square below me. The size of the square resembled what I thought would be the top of the elevator, which made some sense as the place I worked had one fairly close to the front door where I was. I looked and could see more of the area around me. I felt nervous and scared in this area. I had no idea what to do or where to go.

I looked for something familiar that would give me an idea of where I was. I saw nothing: no objects, no calendars, no clocks, no signs of anything to orient myself. I was alone, just alone. At a later date, someone even asked me if I had seen any ladders. I said, "No, I was just alone."

Since I couldn't see any familiar objects, I looked down to see what clothing I had worn. I could still see my outfit from work and my name tag. I think. All of a sudden, I swear I saw my name tag fall off. I was not sure about that, because it dropped too quickly.

But I definitely had the shirt on I had worn to work. At this point, I couldn't see the jeans I had worn; only the shirt.

I looked around for heavenly signs. I saw neither heavenly signs nor heavenly beings such as angels. I didn't see Mary, Joseph, Jesus, or anyone! I did not call for Jesus. I had no idea whether I had arrived at Heaven or if I remained on Earth. I was definitely alone in this area, wherever I was, stuck with nowhere to go.

Not knowing what to do, I looked around and called for family. Strangely enough, I looked up and called for those family members who had died first. I called for Grandma and Grandpa Murphy, Aunt Mary, who was my godmother, Aunt Ann, Uncle Bob, thought about my Grandma Weis, and my brother-in-law, Steve. I'm sure they all prayed for me, but they weren't coming.

I felt desperate when nobody came, so I even called for our family pet, Bailey the dog. I thought I saw him as he started to come through the fog, but then he disappeared behind it. Again, like the name tag, I'm not sure. Everything happened so quickly that I could not know for certain if I saw him or not.

Obviously, my family wasn't coming. Then out of all the people I should have called for on earth, Rod, Mom, Dad, our daughters, why I don't know, but I turned around, in the direction of New Ulm, southwest, and yelled for our parish priest.

Right after I yelled for our priest, I thought, *That was stupid; he's not coming; he's in New Ulm, and I'm at Abbott. That's an hour and a half away. He'll never make it here in time! I know how much priests and pastors affect their parishioners now!*

At this point, I thought I was at Abbott, because that's where the helicopter nurse told me I was going. At least, my last earthly memory was landing at Abbott, but I still didn't know for sure. I couldn't see doctors operating on me or doing anything else to me. I could neither see nor feel anything that was going on with my physical body. I wasn't in any kind of pain.

After I assumed our priest wasn't coming, I didn't know what to do. I waited and waited for something to happen. I felt frustrated and anxious. I didn't know what was going to happen. Although I called for many people, no one came to help. I became very well-aware that **I WAS ALL ALONE. NOBODY CAME TO BAIL ME OUT OR TO SAVE ME FROM THIS AREA; NOT EVEN OUR PRIEST!**

I didn't have a peaceful feeling in this area, probably because I didn't know where I was. I sat there all alone. Maybe a theologian can fill this piece in for me one day. It sure would be nice to know what to call the area where I was.

I felt strange to realize I was out of my body—not somewhere on a trip—but my soul was out of my body, and I was still alive. I had no control over my physical body—let alone my spiritual body. I did not make a conscious choice to go to that area. I didn't tell myself, *I'm going to go have a visit with God today.* It was God's choice.

One thought came to mind about what this area was called. The Catholic Church and the Bible teach us that Jesus descended into Hell for 3 days after He was crucified. Hell is described in the Bible as "the grinding of teeth" or "the fiery furnace". This area wasn't any of those things. I didn't see Satan.

I felt like I experienced Hell because of not knowing where I was or what was going to happen. I was stuck, stuck in an area with nowhere to go. I sat and waited, and waited, and waited. The waiting for something to happen felt like eternity—forever.

All of a sudden, I gasped and wondered if it was my time to die. I became nervous, scared, and sad all at the same time. What about our grandchildren? If it was my time to die, they wouldn't have their Grandma Jean. Plus, I wouldn't be able to spend any more time with them. I wanted to go back, and spend more time with them.

I didn't think I was in Hell because I hadn't died, but I felt scared and it was, as I said, literally, like I experienced *pure Hell.* I thought, *Maybe I'm going to Hell. I didn't know where I was going, but this place could have been Heaven or Hell.*

Then, I wondered, *Is that why I called for our parish priest? Because I thought God was really mad at me, and would send me to Hell for something I had done wrong.* I didn't know what I had done to make

God so mad at me. I was only 52, but maybe if our priest were here, he'd bail me out of this area. Maybe our priest would save me from "the fiery furnace" the Bible calls Hell.

I slowly turned around and gazed up to the Heavens. Looking up, I saw some clouds slowly approaching. They were white, fluffy clouds. They were in a V-formation, much like when geese fly south for the winter.

The clouds moved slowly and stopped overhead. I assumed they were meant for me, but I couldn't be sure. I didn't know what to do or say. I waited for something to happen.

After a bit of silence, a voice said, **"Jean, are you coming?"**

I didn't know who spoke. Since I thought maybe it was my time to die, I made a bold assumption and figured it was God. After all, I was looking up to the Heavens, the direction where I thought God lived, and so I figured it must be God. Besides, I called for others who had died and those still on earth, and none of those people came. I had only one logical conclusion left: The voice was God's.

I felt safe here because I was with God. I knew I was somewhere, and at that point, I decided I wasn't in Hell, because I was with God. I needed to make a decision as to whether I wanted to stay on earth or someplace in Heaven!

In this area where I was, though, I wanted to keep my earthly body.

I wanted to be healthy to go home and back to our grandchildren.

Even though I didn't know it was God, I jumped in and called Him by Name.

I said, "God, could I borrow a little bit more time because our grandchildren need their Grandma Jean?"

I realized Rod and our daughters would be fine if I died; sad for a while, but still fine. I didn't use them as leverage to keep my earthly body. I knew they could take care of themselves.

I had only my grandchildren for bargaining for my life; children come from God. I reasoned, *Maybe with my prayer, God will let me keep my earthly body even if He's really mad at me for something. He might let me stay for them.* I thought I needed to stay on earth for them. I prayed that would be enough for God.

God said, "How much time do you want?"

I thought about how much time I wanted, because I wanted to be specific. At the same time, I didn't want to seem greedy. Our oldest grandchild had started kindergarten. I wanted to see her graduate from kindergarten. I figured that much time wasn't being too greedy.

I said, "Well, maybe enough time to see our oldest grandchild graduate from kindergarten. Then I thought about our second grandchild and added: and maybe see our second grandchild graduate from kindergarten, too."

After that, I stopped. I thought about all the other life events our grandchildren would have, such as graduation from middle school, high school, college, marriage, and having their own children. I wanted to be there for them for those events too. I thought that much time might be too greedy. I justified the time, since it wasn't for me. I wanted to support my grandchildren for as long as possible.

I looked up and said, "And maybe for more time to be there for those life events for them, and for all those life events for any more grandchildren we may have, too?" Again, I wasn't thinking of myself here, I wanted more time, to be fair to all my grandchildren.

God said, **"That much time, huh."**

I continued to look at God. I shrugged my shoulders and didn't say anything more. I waited.

God said, "**Well, what are you going to do for Me?**"

I thought that was a strange question. God should know that I was already doing things for Him, spiritually, that is. I listed all the things I was already doing anyway, since He asked. First, I listed things I had done. I listed that I had volunteered at the clothing depot, and helped clean homes for people in need. Then I stopped; I knew I had done more but that was all I could name.

Then, I listed acts I was doing presently. I listed how I volunteered with the Catholic School's reading program. However, after I started listing those volunteering acts, I stopped.

I thought maybe God was referring to spiritual activities, not volunteering activities. I looked down, and silently listed those spiritual activities. I counted them on my fingers: First, I attended Mass on Sundays and Holy Days. Second, I was a sacristan at our church. Third, I attended adoration once a week. Finally, I prayed the Rosary daily and sometimes even an additional time at the Cathedral.

After I listed those spiritual activities, I stopped. That was it. That was my list. No matter how hard I tried, that was all I could come up with that I had done for God in 52 years: four things. That's not a very long list.

As I reflected on my list, I was disgusted with myself. That short list made me realize that if I were God, I would be disappointed with me.

To redeem myself, I tried to name more things I would do in order to keep my earthly body. As I started thinking of more acts I could do, I stopped. I thought there was no way I could fit anything more into my schedule. Besides, I didn't know what this **more was** that I was going to do. I hadn't considered replacing or making changes to things that already kept me busy.

I certainly didn't want to promise I was going to do anything for God and then not do it. To me, if I made a promise to someone and didn't follow through, that would be considered a sin.

Mom and Dad always said, "If you say you are going to do something for anyone, unless an emergency comes up, you should always do it. Otherwise, how does anyone learn to trust you? After that lesson from Mom and Dad, I always tried to be a concrete person that way. Besides, they were right. It wouldn't take me long to learn to distrust people, if they continuously went back on their words.

I didn't want God to think He couldn't trust me. I reasoned that *God would take me if He thought he couldn't trust me. After all, why would God want someone on earth if He couldn't trust them?*

I needed to come up with an answer for God. He was waiting. My answer had to be so great that there was no way God would refuse to let me keep my earthly body. While I talked to God, I heard a song with a few particular phrases. One phrase was about never ceasing to worship God and the other phrase was that even the mountains bowed down in God's name. I recognized the lyrics, but couldn't remember the name of the song and didn't know why I heard those phrases now. Slowly, the song started to come through louder and louder.

While I listened to this song, I thought, maybe there's still a chance to keep my earthly body with the things I was already doing. God hadn't taken me yet. I was still here somewhere. Somebody was singing those words for a reason. I didn't know who or why, but they were sung from above. There wasn't anybody around, and I couldn't actually see anybody. All I heard were the singing voices.

Finally, without knowing what I was going to say, I realized I had to hurry up and say something, because, like I said, I was afraid God was going to take me. So, I turned around, looked up, and gave God the answer to His question, **"What are you going to do for Me**?"

I responded, "I could still become a better person."

After that, I stopped, embarrassingly looked down, and thought, *That's it? That's the great answer I came up with for God? That I could still become a better person?* I felt sad because I thought that was a stupid answer, and I didn't think that answer was good enough for God. It was a pretty vague response. The only thingI could state specifically I was going to do for God was that I could still become a better person. I thought, *Great, now what!*

God was obviously deciding what to do now since He was silent for a while. I felt like I needed something ***more*** to keep my earthly body, but I didn't know what. I waited and prayed now for something. Whatever this ***more*** was I needed, I knew it wasn't going to come from me. I did all I could do. Finally, to my surprise, what I needed to keep my earthly body came.

Suddenly, I heard more voices. I turned around and looked in the direction from where I heard them. It was in the same direction

I had turned to when I yelled for our parish priest: southwest, New Ulm. Those voices mumbled quietly at first as if off in the distance.I couldn't tell who or what they said. The voices came through in an outline in the form of heads like that of a silhouette, much like what a kindergartner draws of them self. The sound of mumbling came in a lower tone than the others singing from above.

I realized those voices might be people on earth who heard about my condition by now and were praying for me. Maybe, in a way, the singing from above and the mumbling of voices were prayers. I didn't know for sure if they were prayers, because I couldn't tell what they were singing or saying, and I didn't know what I had done to deserve all their prayers. After all, I had named only four things that I had done for God in 52 years. I wondered why would all those people be praying for me, when all I had done for God were four things.

I tried to justify to myself (while keeping God waiting, mind you) why those people might be praying for me. I belonged to a church. Some people knew me from church. Maybe those people were praying for me, and prayer was what I needed to keep my earthly body. Maybe those prayers would be enough for God to let me keep my earthly body.

As I realized those voices might be people who prayed for me, I turned around, looked up at God, and said, **"Look, I think they're praying for me!"**

ALL PRAYERS mean something to God. I could tell those prayers meant something to God, too. As I looked to the clouds from where I heard God's voice, they moved in the same direction as more mumbling silhouettes came through. That's how I knew God heard all who prayed for me.

God said, "**Well, okay. I'll give you another chance.**"

I gave a silent prayer of thanks and a sigh of relief.

I quickly started back into the square which was the same one from which I had come. I didn't want God to change His mind about giving me another chance. I was half-way down and then I thought, Wait! Maybe I should ask one more question. I figured I better ask as long as I was there! (Really, like I have been in this spot before? C'mon!)

Sometimes when I'm in trouble, I make deals with somebody and then wish I hadn't. I hate to admit that when I was with God, that happened to me. Since I wanted to have another chance at life, I didn't want to screw this up.

Football season was underway before my heart attack.

Those who know me, know I am a big Green Bay Packer fan having been born and raised in Wisconsin, until 1979. After I graduated from high school in Prairie du Chien Wisconsin, Dad moved us to Bemidji, Minnesota to serve as a director of a treatment center for children ages 8-18, who were emotionally disturbed.

One of the values the Green Bay Packer fans were to have as taught by one of their earlier coaches, Vince Lombardi was loyalty.

I really didn't like the idea of switching team loyalties at this stage of my life, but because I wanted to keep my earthly body, I figured I'd ask. I decided if I had to switch team loyalties and be a Minnesota Viking fan, I'd switch so I could live longer. Switching loyalties, to me, was better than being dead.

After I realized God was going to let me keep my earthly body, instead of being grateful for that, I asked for more.

I looked up at God and said: "God, you know that part about being a better person?"

God said, **"Yes."**

I said, "Does that mean I have to be a Minnesota Viking fan?"

Seriously, I should have asked about how to achieve world peace or something other than the Green Bay Packers, but no, instead of that, I ask about the Green Bay Packers. Geez! Oh well, what could I do now?

I knew God would never create anything evil, and I was sure that was a stupid question, but I figured I'd better check as long as I was there. Again, I didn't want to screw up this second chance of life.

God said, "**No, but you have to be a GOOD Green Bay Packer fan.**"

I thought God's answer was odd as I thought I was already a pretty good Packer fan, but I figured okay, I'd keep that in mind. After all, another value of being a good Packer fan anyway was being a good sport. When new people wanted to know more about me, I always told them, "I'll make it quick. I'm a Catholic-born-Wisconsin native-German-Irish-Swiss-Luxembourger-Green-Bay-Packer fan!" That statement pretty much summed up my upbringing, values, interests, and pastimes. Everyone usually laughs at the phrase and groans when it comes to the Packer fan part!

Ironically here, I thought of the time when Mom and Dad moved our family from Prairie du Chien, Wisconsin, to Bemidji, MN. On the way to Bemidj, I worried about being a Packer fan in Minnesota, because of the loyalty value the Packer team taught. I wanted to remain loyal to the Packer team while living in Minnesota. I asked Dad the same question I asked God.... and his answer was the same as Gods'!

One would think that question would be enough, but no, I continued to ask more questions! I thought about all the other Packer fans in New Ulm, and wanted to be sure it was okay for them to be Packer fans, too.

I looked up and said, "How about all the other Green Bay Packer fans in New Ulm?" I had it in the back of my mind that I had to be loyal to the team and defend the fans.

God said, "**Yes, they can keep being Green Bay Packer fans, but they have to be good ones, too!**"

Then I gave another sigh of relief and said, "Thank you!" Then I started going back down into a tunnel or the same dark square from which I came.

At this point, I must have tried to connect with my earthly body. This is difficult to explain. I remember falling through space really fast and trying to wake up. The pace was so fast that I don't remember my being in a tunnel. When I was almost back, I looked up and could see the white lights in the hospital room (yes, these were the lights in the room) and the white part of the sleeve of the cloak on the priest's arm.

I thought the priest was giving me my Last Rights, because I heard him mumbling something and felt him put holy oil on my forehead or holy water. At this same time, I tried to tell him to stop that (putting oils on my head and saying prayers) because I didn't need it anymore. I wasn't in my physical body yet, when I said this. I was coming back and looking up seeing the priest administer those rights to me! It was freaky! After I told the priest to stop— that I didn't need it anymore— I felt him put oil on my forehead, and I went out again; gratefully knowing I was on earth.

Later, my husband verified that the priest was giving me the Anointing of the Sick, not my Last Rights. After an explanation of the Anointing of the Sick, Rod said, "It's different than the Last Rights, because the priest wanted you to get well and did not assume you were going to die."

The Anointing of the Sick sometimes heals. Rod said, "During the process, your eyes became huge." Maybe this happened when I tried to tell the priest to "stop that" when I was coming back. I asked Rod to clarify how my eyes became huge. He said, "I don't know how to explain it. They just got huge." Gratefully, at this point, I knew I was in my earthly body again and blessed to have more time with our grandchildren.

CHAPTER 3:

EARTH?

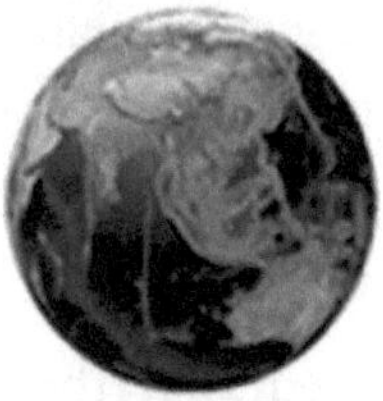

When I woke up and knew I was back on earth, I heard people in the room. I heard my husband in the background, and our youngest daughter, Rose. I tried to call for Rod right away, but nothing came out. Then I heard Rose telling me, "Mom, the hard part's over." I thought to myself, *What hard part? I'm here.* When I slowly became more alert, I could see what she meant: I was hooked up to many machines and doctors and nurses were all around me.

My husband told me right away that he loved me. I remember telling him, "I'm scared, I don't want to die," as tears rolled down my face. Then I said, "I love you," and repeated the phrase, "I don't want to die." When I saw everyone around me, I told Rod, "I'm scared. I don't want to be all this trouble." He reassured me that I was fine, and that I was not any trouble.

Rod told me that my vitals were being taken often and they were okay. He told me how I was at the best heart hospital in the world. He also said, "Your physician, Dr. Frannie Knowles in New Ulm, is already on your case." For some reason, that made me feel much better.

I heard my brother-in-law's voice. He found out about my heart attack from my sister, Jill. They live in Arizona. He "happened" to be in the Cities for business, dropped everything and came to see me.

Clark looked at me, and I held on to his hand for dear life! There was no way I was going to let him go. Finally, he said, "Jean, I have to go and catch my plane, okay!" I cried and he said, "Keep up the good fight."

Friends of ours from Fosston, Minnesota stopped in on their way to the airport. Joann and Dale have been friends of ours, since before we were married. They learned about my situation from a phone call they received from another friend of ours in Fosston, we've known over 30 years-Lorinda. I could barely see Joann or Dale. Dale was very silent. Joann spoke first.

Joann said, "Jean, we just stopped by to say hi, and we bought you a Green Bay Packer mug, because we know you're such a big Green Bay fan, okay?"

I tried to tell them thank you, but I couldn't say anything. I started to cry, because I couldn't thank them or let them know how appreciative I was that they came, and that I was okay. Finally, I shook my head yes, so they knew I could hear them.

The Green Bay mug was the first gift I received. From that, I made a direct connection that my conversation with God about the Packers was REAL! I was relieved because I knew I was with God.

My throat was sore, as I had evidently pulled out my breathing tube (which I don't remember). Rod repeated the same phrases over and over until I realized where I was. I was so scared that I, too, repeated my questions and comments about my fear of dying. We consoled one another during that whole time.

My family also told me how the nurses and doctors said what a miracle I was. They also told me that every cardiologist who came in to see me raved about the care from the New Ulm Medical Center. The most common phrase I heard from my family was that every cardiologist who came into my room said,

"Had the New Ulm Medical Center not done what they did in that ER room or even lagged on one step, basically, Jean wouldn't be here."

I wasn't quite sure what my family meant at first about this miracle business because I wasn't sure where I was yet, after I regained consciousness: here or back with God. After I heard the comments about the great care that the New Ulm Medical Center gave me, over and over, I wondered if I was really that close to death?

Those positive comments from my family about our medical center made me realize how blessed I was that I was in New Ulm, Minnesota. The more I heard those positive comments about the care and expertise I received from the New Ulm Medical Center from my family, the more appreciative I became of the work the doctors and nurses had done for me.

I wondered if the New Ulm Medical Center ever heard anything about their good works from anyone. I wanted to find a way to tell the doctors and nurses at the medical center that their hard work was noticed, appreciated, and recognized by major hospitals. All the cardiologists at Abbott, instead of giving themselves the credit for my survival, gave it to the New Ulm Medical Center:

THANK YOU, ABBOTT, FOR DOING THAT!

I wanted to make a difference somehow for the center and the community. I didn't know how I could make a difference, but the New Ulm Medical Center saved me, and even though I think I'm not a very important person, I'm just a Catholic-born-Wisconsin native-German-Irish- Swiss-Luxembourger-Green Bay Packer fan; I'm a person. A life should count for something. Maybe, I could still do something good.

Remembering my visit with God, I wondered if I was really with Him. But from the comments my family made about our medical center, and as I remembered my visit with God, I realized I was definitely somewhere else. And wherever it was, it was not on Earth. I didn't know where I was. But wherever I was or whatever the place was called, it existed! It wasn't a dream or figment of my imagination. God was there with me!

During the time I became more alert, I could see my name bracelet on my wrist, which told me who I was, etc. and on my stent card was Dr. Tim Henry's name, my surgeon. I wondered where he was. I wanted to meet, and thank him, but everyone told me that he left. I thought maybe people meant that he left for the day, but evidently, he had taken a chief position as a cardiologist somewhere out in California, and left permanently.

I felt cheated about not being able to thank him, and I thought, *no, I never said thank you, but I figured he must be needed out there now. I was grateful to have had him when I needed him.* He was flying back and forth yet, from California to Minnesota and had two weeks left in Minneapolis when I came. He "happened" to be on call! Yep, the top cardiologist at Abbott happened to be on call! I don't think that was a coincidence!

At that point, when I learned that Dr. Henry was gone, Rod found Chaplain John, who came to see me. He was concerned about me as I was still telling people I didn't want to die.

Chaplain John said, "Jean, who told you, you were going to die?" I could sense people were worried about this.

I said, "Nobody!"

I thought that I should quit saying I was going to die, and I kept that to myself. After all, I couldn't even explain to anyone what happened, let alone where I was. Plus, I was at Abbott. The last thing I needed was to have people start thinking I was a nut because nobody knew me, and because I kept telling Rod I didn't want to die. I also didn't want to end up seeing some psych doctor and taking longer to go home.

I thought, *Great! Who am I going to talk to about this?* I thought, maybe I could talk to the Chaplain, but I decided I didn't want to push my luck. He was not an ordained priest. Chaplain John was kind and comforting.

Chaplain John said, "Is there anything we can do for you?" I responded, "Can I have a Confession?"

He said, "Sure, let me find Fr. John."

In the Catholic religion, ordained priests are the people who can hear confessions. I didn't know what to think about this experience, and I considered the fact that I might be a nut. I didn't know if this experience was real! I didn't plan this experience, and I thought I had committed a mortal sin—in our Catholic religion, a mortal sin would separate me from God, *FOREVER! I would have no chance to go to Heaven.*

I feared I would end up in Hell, because I had never heard of anything like this experience happening to anyone! I knew I had the sacrament of Confession to rely on now that I was back, and I wanted to make darn sure I was as close to God as I could be, before I died again. This sacrament was going to do that: bail me out of whatever this sin was I may have committed.

Then, I thought twice about going to Confession. An ordained priest might think a person was confused when a parishioner told him that she/he lied to God, when she/he was with Him. WITH HIM! I certainly didn't want to be held responsible for telling a lie, especially in Confession, when I didn't plan my experience. I thought if I told a lie in Confession, I'd have to go to Confession again!

Not only did I not know what to think about this experience, I didn't even know how to say it. How do I tell anyone of the experience of my visit with God, let alone, someone I didn't know, even if I was in Confession with an ordained priest, without them thinking I was a nut?

After my experience, I knew I would definitely talk to my priest about this. I knew I needed to go to Confession now. I wanted to wait until I was home, and be with someone who I was comfortable talking to about my experience.

By the time Fr. John came, I had become more aware of my physical connection to my body and thought, *I know this experience happened, and I won't second-guess myself.* I wondered how I might skip this confession. I thought it was not a big deal to skip Confession anyway. I had skipped it for years myself! Thankfully, by the time Fr. John came, the subject of a Confession didn't come up. I thought, *Whew, I dodged that bullet!* He brought Communion to me, which I enthusiastically received.

I didn't know what my husband thought about these spiritual experiences or whatever this was, so I decided not to tell him yet. I wasn't even sure whether I would tell him. I would wait until I had more information and talk to a friend of mine. Now, my goal became to focus on my wellness, and going home.

After I realized many peoples' prayers had helped me keep my earthly body, my goal grew. I wanted to thank the New Ulm Medical Center and the entire community.

I thought about all the care Abbott gave me. I added Abbott to my goal in thanking people. They probably heard thanks all the time, because they are a major heart hospital in Minnesota, but I wanted to thank them personally. My goal in thanking people for my well-being continued to grow.

I was amazed to learn how many people were involved to help make me well, the medical expertise of the New Ulm Medical Center, Abbott, peoples' prayers, and the Anointing of the Sick that Fr. John performed on me brought me back.

I had done nothing to deserve all this care. God was still deciding what to do with me until all those prayers started coming through; and it was then that I said to God, *Look, I think they're all praying for me*! It was then that God decided and said, **"Okay, I'll give you another chance."**

Another goal for getting well, too, was maybe I could find someone to talk to about this experience I had at Abbott. I needed the right person though. I figured whoever this person at Abbott might be, at least, if I were well, I wouldn't be judged and sent to the psych ward!

However, I decided against telling anyone at Abbott about my experience. I didn't want to push my luck. I decided to wait until

I was home to talk to someone. I would focus on getting well and going home. That's it: getting well and going home!

This type of wellness could only happen (as my husband, Rod put it) from "the best heart hospital in the world!"

Chapter 4:

Abbott Northwestern Heart Hospital Minneapolis, Minnesota

Many doctors came and went, doing different tests, taking labs vitals, and trying to get me well. The first doctor I remember was the neurologist. He came in to do some tests to see if I had had a stroke. That may have been the same afternoon I woke up.

My family was there too.

He asked me general questions at first. Dr: "Where are you?"

Me: "Abbott."

Dr: "Do you remember what happened?"

Me: "I had a heart attack." (Everyone seemed pretty excited about this.)

Dr: "What year is it?" Me: "2013."

Dr: "What month is it?" Me: "August."

Dr: "Do you remember what day of the week it is?"

The last day I remembered was Monday when I was at work and the whole ambulance trip. I drew a blank here regarding today's day because I wasn't sure. I had tears rolling down my face because I was afraid of what would happen when I told them I couldn't remember the day. I couldn't even guess at what the day was, so I shook my head no.

The doctor turned to my family and said that was pretty typical right after waking. I was relieved when I heard him tell my family that not remembering the day was normal, because, at least, he wouldn't think I was a nut!

Then he told me, "Jean, it's Wednesday, August 28."

I couldn't believe it was two days later from my memories of Monday. I knew I was with God, but to me, it was a short visit. Not only that, I didn't remember sleeping, eating or anything when I was with God. So, for two days, I was awake the whole time. I'm pretty sure I couldn't stay awake for two days down here. I started to get teary-eyed as I realized that two days were lost out of my life.

More importantly, today was our oldest grandchild's birthday and first day of school. I had planned to go with her, her mother, and her younger sister! I felt like I disappointed her missing her birthday, and first day of school special. But what could I do? God obviously had other plans for me.

Two whole days! Two days that I didn't know anything that happened around me, and that I relied on strangers to take care of me, and follow through with my end of life issues, and needs. The neurologist continued with his questioning.

Dr: "Who is the president?"

Me: "Obama." (I gave him a disgusting sort of glance as I'm not a fan but knew I better answer correctly. Everyone kind of chuckled at that.)

Then the next set of questions came. He said he was going to give me three words and wanted me to repeat them. I did, forward and backward. He determined I didn't have a stroke, but it would take a while to regain my strength. He was going to come back and do another set of tests in a couple days. I thought, *Yeah! One doctor done!*

Next, I needed an MRI. Since I couldn't move on my own yet, nurses transferred me to a table with an electric lift, which is a big deal. I wanted to get out of Abbott, so I cooperated as best as I could.

The MRI was frightening. I felt like I was going into a big coffin; literally! After almost dying, this terrified me. With the hot flashes that came on in there, and the loud noises of the MRI, I panicked! I prayed for a quick ending.

I could hear the technician's voice, so, gratefully, I knew she was still in the room with me. The last thing I wanted was to be stuck in this coffin with no way out, especially if the technician had disappeared, gone to another room or died herself.

When the technician finished, I told her what happened about how I panicked. When she heard this, she mentioned something about why I didn't use a button. I gave her a confused look when she said this and didn't know what to say.

After she saw my face, she realized something happened where I couldn't call. Then she asked if I had a panic button. I said, "No." She felt terrible. Thankfully, though, we figured it out.

During the MRI process, too, there was a break. I asked her about this break, because it felt like it lasted for an eternity. She explained later that it was only 3 minutes, so she could check the results.

When she heard that the break to me felt like an eternity, she felt worse. She said she'd remember those two things next time: the panic button and checking on patients to keep them informed of what would happen.

The next doctor was a speech pathologist. She was very nice and extremely calming. She worked on teaching me to swallow, so I could take my medications orally, which would be more effective. Sheoffered me different types of sherbet. I chose orange. I tried swallowing, and I spit it out right away. I was surprised at how awful the sherbet (because I love sherbet) tasted, and how hard it was to swallow.

Tears started rolling down my cheeks again. I wasn't sure what was going to happen next. Worse than that, since I couldn't swallow, I thought maybe it was going to take longer for me to go home.

A new nurse came for the next shift. She explained to me thatsince I didn't pass the swallowing test, she needed to put in a feeding tube.

She said, "I hate to do this. I asked two doctors to change their minds, but they wouldn't. The meds are pretty important, so I need to put in this tube, and it has to go down your nose."

I said, "Okay" and thought, *inserting this tube through my nose can't be that bad.* She told me to cough, as she and two others inserted the tube. I didn't like that idea but tried to cooperate as best as I could. I didn't want to die, and wanted to go home, so I would do anything they asked.

During the process of inserting the feeding tube in my nose, I felt like I was going to choke, and I couldn't breathe. Those feelings were so horrible that I automatically pulled out the tube. The nurses were disappointed at my reaction, but gave me time to re-group. Theydidn't realize, of course, that I had had a visit with God.

I'm sure my visit with God had a lot to do with my reaction to the feeding tube, and the need for wanting to pull it out. The experience of choking was so strong that I couldn't control pulling it out. My reaction was instantaneous. Now, I prayed they wouldn't have to try to put the tube back in through my nose.

The speech pathologist came back when she heard what happened with my feeding tube. She said she'd talk to the doctors, and see if they could wait until tomorrow as one more day made such a difference in recovery.

I thought, *Whew, maybe I'll get lucky.* I was pretty close to passing the swallowing test, and she didn't want me to have a feeding tube if I didn't need it. Neither did the other nurses, but they were more apt to go with the doctors, I suppose.

By the next day, I was able to swallow, so the doctors determined the feeding tube wasn't necessary. *YEAH! Now, I had one more doctor out of the way, and I was that much closer to going home.*

I saw an occupational therapist the next day (the 29th). She administered a couple tests to check my reflexes and fine motor skills. By now, I was stronger, and she felt comfortable with what I had accomplished, so she didn't take me through the whole process. She knew I had been through enough.

The occupational therapist said I was doing so well, and she couldn't figure out why, especially after what I had been through. She came back two days later to check on me, and crossed me off her list. *YEAH! ONE MORE DOCTOR OUT OF THE WAY AND CLOSER TO GOING HOME! THANK YOU!*

The nurses were imperative now that I start moving. I was feeling better, and wanted to try to sit up anyway. I sat up and made it for about half an hour the first time. That felt strange, but good to sit up in bed. After I finished, I napped for a couple hours. It was a big feat evidently, sitting up and being out of bed for the first time. After all, I had 7 stents placed in me and was told this procedure had never been done to the point of someone surviving! It probably stands to reason that I was tired enough to take a nap for a couple hours after I sat up for the first time.

I remembered being nervous, as I sat up in bed the first time. Later that evening, I tried again, though, to build some strength. I sat up during my whole meal. I don't remember what my first meal was, but probably chicken broth and tea. I started to feel less anxious about my visit with God, but still kept it quiet from others.

I remembered continuing to hear those phrases from that song about *all that I am…* A little more to the song started to come through. I started telling myself I have to figure out the message, and rest of the words to that song when I'm home. Otherwise, it was (guess what, yep), going to drive me nuts!

During all those tests, the lab ladies came, too.

I finally decided to ask one of them, "What are you checking me for?"

Lab Tech said, "Potassium."

I said, "Oh? Why?"

Lab Tech said, "Because your potassium level is low and that is what caused you to be out for two days after your stenting procedure. The doctors want your level to be within normal limits before sending you home. When your potassium level stabilizes, you'll be closer to going home."

After I heard her explanation of why my potassium levels needed to stabilize, I decided to order bananas to boost up my potassium level, and it worked. I learned about this banana tip to improve my potassium levels from my physician with a previous condition I had. Yes, I'm sure glad our DOCTORS IN NEW ULM, MINNESOTA know what they're doing!

My arms were so sore from all the needles, the lab technicians were to a point that one of them used a latex glove, put warm water in it, and placed the glove on one of the areas from where she could draw blood. This was a great idea and, frankly, felt kind of good. The last lab draw was Saturday, August 29, 2013, (that week). *YEAH! ONE MORE TEST DONE AND CLOSER TO GOING HOME!*

The following day, the nurses came in, and asked if I wanted to take a phone call. They felt bad about waking me so early, but the person kept calling, and was insistent about talking to me. I said, "Sure! I'm up anyway." The caller was our friend Russ in Fosston who farms.

I said, "Only you would call me at 6:30 in the morning." He harassed me and said, "Well, you answered!"

I teased Russ and said, "I had to. They told me you had called a couple times already!"

We had a nice visit, and it felt like yesterday that we had talked.

After we hung up, one of the nurses came back to do vitals. I said, "Sorry about that. Those Fosston people do a lot of farming, and are up early." She laughed.

The neurologist came back today, too. He needed another round of testing done to determine if I was stronger. Interestingly, I recuperated rather quickly. I think I recuperated so quickly because of my own mindset of wanting to go home, and more importantly, *it was because of the prayers I still received and didn't even know about yet. They enabled me to get better.*

Unfortunately, I had a setback. One of the cardiologists came, and explained that my previous MRI showed another hole in my heart and an extra flap, he called it. They needed to do another MRI. The cardiologist said, "If the issues they were checking didn't come from the heart attack, then they'd leave it alone. However, if they came from the heart attack then I'd require more surgery, but that would come later. Since it was a holiday weekend, they wanted to do the MRI that day, and then, if all went well, perhaps I could move to the fifth floor, maybe even today".

Being transferred to the fifth floor was a big deal, Since, once I was up there, I'd go home in a couple days.

I thought, Oh, no! If I'm going to have another surgery, it's going to be while I'm here now. I'm not coming back to this place. Ever! Obviously, I would if I had another heart issue, but it wasn't going to be anytime soon.

I was reluctant about having another MRI, since the first time around didn't go so well.

I said, "I'm scared."

The cardiologist reassured me and said, "We'll all be right here with you."

To have extra security, my husband and daughter came with me. Actually, I insisted that they come! I didn't want to be stuck in that machine without any way out. Plus, I wanted someone there in case the technician or someone else out there died. I know that reasoning was foolish, as we all know God has the final call in our lives anyway. But, after all, I almost died, and came back, so I knew firsthand about surviving something like this, whatever *this* was.

Two nurses prepared and wheeled me on a gurney once again down to the MRI room. I told them how scared I was, too. They tried to reassure me but didn't know how. Finally, I quit saying that, because I could tell they were nervous. I could even see on my care board one issue in declaring me well was to reduce anxiousness.

When I saw that reducing my anxiousness was a factor in determining my wellness to go home, I thought, *Gee, you think I'm anxious. C'mon, I almost died, had a visit with God even, and you wondered why I'm anxious? I thought if they only knew the whole story!* I tried to co-operate the best I could, so I could go home.

This time, the MRI wasn't as bad, because I knew what to expect and had extra security. I had my panic button, and pretended to be calm so they would quit calling me anxious. Then maybe they'd finish the testing faster, so I could go home.

At the end, the cardiologist came out, and determined the extra flap and hole in my heart were from birth, so they didn't have to do any further surgeries! *YEAH! One more test out of the way and closer to going home.*

The last test, so to speak, was having a bowel movement before moving to the fifth floor. The prescription of three Senna tabs proved effective, as my nurse visited me quite often that night! Now, I could move up to the fifth floor!

By Saturday, August 31, 2013, things calmed down, visitors started to come, and people continued to call. This amazed me because, after all, it's just me, a Catholic-born-Wisconsin-native-German-Irish-Swiss-Luxembourger-Green Bay Packer fan. I couldn't believe all those people came to see me. I have no clout or status. Who am I to be so blessed with all those visitors who came, and more importantly, prayed for me?

Since most of the testing was done, I recuperated and rested until I could go home. My next and final stop at Abbott was the fifth floor. When I moved up there, I knew I would be going home soon.

My daughter, Rose, had left a list of questions for the cardiologist when he returned. She left it with me to be sure I'd learn what I needed to do when I went home. When I looked at the questions one of them was explaining more what SCAD was. I thought, *SCAD? What was that and who had it?*

Suddenly, it dawned on me that I must have had SCAD. I repeated *SCAD.* That didn't even sound nice. I wondered what I did to get that?

When the next cardiologist came in during routine rounds, he asked if there was anything he could do. That was the same cardiologist who visited with my family after my surgery.

Finally, being braver, I gave him the list of questions Rose had and asked, **"What is this SCAD?"**

The cardiologist replied, "SCAD is Spontaneous Coronary Artery Dissection. It's very rare, and we truly only get 3 to 5 cases a year." He explained that SCAD is found in women in their early 50s going through menopause or their early 30s who are pregnant. We guess it's a hormone, but we don't know which one because we don't have enough cases to do studies with."

After he said that, I thought to myself, *Huh? What? You guys are Abbott, and I can't imagine you had to* ***guess*** *at anything! You're supposed to know these issues, instinctively!* People forget how human doctors are! After all, if they were gods, we'd live forever, right? We wouldn't have to ask God if we could borrow more time!

The doctor repeated what my family told me about the care I received from the New Ulm Medical Center:

"Had New Ulm not done what they did, you wouldn't be here."

I asked, "Everyone had told me how my leg was just shaking after the operation. Is this typical?"

The cardiologist replied, "Yes, it's typical after that kind of operation. The nurses held your leg so you wouldn't bleed out."

After I heard his explanation of the results of my procedure, and the rarity of my condition, I wondered if my visit with God was one of those experiences people talked about like in that movie *Heaven Is For Real*? I wasn't about to ask, though.

I really had no idea how to ask him about any of this, because I didn't even know what my experience with God was. I knew doctors, generally speaking, were more into the science end of things, so I decided not to ask. The last thing I wanted was for any one at Abbott to think I was a nut!

After he assumed I was satisfied with that explanation of my illness, he continued by telling me about the meds I would be on, and asked if I needed to hear about the risks versus benefits of them. I said no, because I had dealt with that issue thousands of times when I worked at the group home, so I understood what he was saying about them. I thanked him for his time before he left.

Besides, he was a cardiologist, and I knew he was busy. I also needed time to let all this information sink in, and figure out what to do with my experience. Before he left, he repeated what my family had said about the New Ulm Medical Center and told me, as though to confirm the message, **"Had New Ulm not done what they did, you wouldn't be here."**

I didn't know much about those experiences I had. I always believed in God, angels, Jesus, Heaven, and the charismatic realm, but this experience was way over my head. Because of the cardiologist's explanation of the rarity of my condition, I realized *more-than-ever* how close to death I had come, and that something uniquely different had happened to me.

I had heard about people dying and being brought back to life. That was as much as I knew about those kinds of experiences. I didn't know anything happened to the soul of a person during that time.

Now though, I definitely knew there was something that happened to me when I was gone. The experience I had was real; **very, very real.** It was freaky. I just didn't know what to call it or what to do with it.

Part of the reason I didn't know what to call my experience was, because I still didn't realize the whole connection between the physical and spiritual aspects of the persons involved. I knew SCAD was rare, but Near-Death Experiences— *to me*— was a term signifying that a doctor had actually called the person dead with whatever medical condition he/she had.

Nobody at the hospital would mention or admit the remotest possibility that I had died. Nobody used the term **dying** when they were talking to me about my condition. They spoke only about what had happened.

When doctors explained my situation, they actually avoided using the terms **death** or **dying**, although I had been that close to death. They stayed with purely medical terms. The explanation of the rarity of my condition that the doctors gave me seemed bizarre, because it appeared as though they wanted to add something else, but couldn't make themselves say whatever they were holding back.

Interestingly, though, every time cardiologists came in to see me at Abbott, I felt like they were looking at me as if I were some kind of ghost. The expressions on their faces scared me. The expressions on their face were uncanny and somehow blank. I don't know how else to describe it. Consequently, I wasn't about to ask any of them about my experience. I only wanted to go home.

On the other side, the clergy at the hospital didn't know what I had encountered during those two days that I was unconscious, so they couldn't name my experience for me. There was no way I was going to try to explain it to them. After all, why would any clergy, who didn't know me, believe anything I said. Sure! Clergy should believe in those kinds of issues, but they weren't going to hear it from me. I didn't tell them, because I didn't want them to keep me in the hospital any longer than I had to be! They didn't know me from Adam!

I suspect that Chaplain John sensed something happened because at one point he asked me, "Who told you that you were going to die?"

I hesitated then told him, "Nobody."

I sensed that he was nervous about my continued asking of that question. He could tell that I had encountered something that I didn't want to share with him. I kept my experience to myself, so, to him the clergy, it didn't exist because I wasn't going to tell them about it.

At the time of my heart attack (I'll call it SCAD from now on), the movie *Heaven Is for Real* was released. All anybody had told me about that movie was that it was about a little boy who died, went to Heaven, and came back. I didn't doubt the story. The boy died, and came back. That's the only kind of knowledge I had with anything of this spiritual nature. I thought about going to the movie, but I decided against it. Besides, I didn't have the time. It also didn't affect me… much.

When that movie came out, I figured because of the sensitivity of the material, it must be about a family who was quite influential for a movie to be made of them and so widely accepted. Otherwise, how else could a person convince anyone this kind of event happened?

Those experiences, like in the movie *Heaven Is for Real* (to me), were designed by God with the intent to share and convince others that God and Heaven EXIST! Those experiences, therefore, seemed to be given to people with clout, people who have lots of money and status, people who have a position of power within their employment, so the person who went through such an experience could easily convince others that God and Heaven ARE real.

I was certainly not a person with clout, who could easily convince others I was in Heaven and that God and Heaven existed! Since I believed I had never had any clout or status in my life, I felt I would never have any impact on other adults.

I wasn't sure who to ask that would come up with a concrete term for my experience, but I decided to ask my dear and trusted friend of ten years plus, Mary Kay. She would be honest enough to let me know if what I had experienced had a name. She might even tell me whom to ask for that information.

Having this experience surprised me, because I already believed in God, Heaven, Jesus, and all the angels and saints, but I didn't think this would happen to me! After all, I'm just a Catholic-born-Wisconsin-native-German-Irish-Swiss-Luxembourger-Green Bay Packer fan, who didn't seem to have any clout or status. To me, I'm a normal, average, everyday person, who believed in God and Heaven already! How was *I, by myself,* going to convince anyone that God and Heaven truly existed.

More importantly, *why me*? Why on earth would God have chosen *me* to do this: to convince others He and Heaven Exist; to do this great feat? I'm a behind-the-scenes kind of person. I work without fanfare. WHY ME? Yeah, right!

I stopped being worried about convincing people about God, and set out for my next course of action. My immediate goal was to do something for the New Ulm Medical Center and the community, because of the cardiologist's explanation of the rarity of my condition. *I wanted to let everyone in the whole-wide world to know that the New Ulm Medical Center, although relatively small, has doctors who know what they're doing!*

I also knew that my survival was the mutual effort of both hospitals and their staffs. I realized only later that the third part of the triangle was the spiritual part: prayers from those who loved me, prayers for those who cared about me, and prayers from strangers who had heard about me. I was amazed to learn this. And it was overwhelming, too!

I figured by now I must have had this experience to share this with others: that God and Heaven exist— they truly exist! I thought the community, and others should know what their prayers had done and what happened. Everyone had as big a part in saving my life. I had to tell everyone that their prayers were heard by God and that they worked. What a person does on earth really does matter! My experience was for others. That's it. It was meant to share with others! I needed to convince everyone that:

GOD HEARD THEIR PRAYERS AND THEIR PRAYERS WORKED— AND GOD AND HEAVEN EXIST! THEY TRULY

EXIST! *It's not just a story in the Bible; they truly EXIST!*

I wanted people to know their prayers were heard so they would keep praying for others.

After I talked to my friend, and had a name for my experience, then, I'd talk to our priest about it. Maybe that is why I called for him during my two-day encounter with God. I wanted an explanation about what I had experienced. I knew he wouldn't think I was a nut anyway. I didn't know him personally at all, but he knew me as a volunteer and a parishioner. I like to be safe at times like these.

I decided okay, I'll wait for a Confession until I went home. I prayed I'd be safe from dying until I had a Confession. It was an awful feeling, though, not being able to talk to anyone. Now, I was more determined to start focusing on my wellness, and going home.

At that point, I still couldn't understand what I had done to deserve all those prayers, but I knew they were all heard and that they worked. Without the work of the doctors and all those prayers, I wouldn't be here. I tried to think of something, somehow, someway to thank everyone for all their prayers, and to let them know that their prayers were heard and that they worked for me and helped!

CHAPTER 5:

VISITORS

PLEASE REMEMBER: PRAYERS ARE ALWAYS HEARD AND THEY WORK! THOSE WHO PRAY ARE VERY IMPORTANT TO GOD AND SO ARE THOSE FOR WHOM THEY PRAY. ONLY GOD KNOWS WHAT THAT PERSON IS GOING THROUGH OR WHAT THAT PERSON NEEDS. PRAYER IS WHAT TRULY BRINGS PEOPLE BACK FROM THE BRINK OF ETERNITY. PRAYER LETS THEM KNOW THEY'RE IMPORTANT, AND HAVE A REASON TO BE ALIVE AND COME BACK.

Our daughter, Louise, and her husband, Bruce, came Friday night with our two grandchildren. Everyone seemed nervous, especially their daughter, Lola, who had never seen me that way: all hooked up to machines. I would have left Lola home. She was pretty young to understand what was happening to her Grandma Jean. It was great therapy for me, though.

Bruce asked Lola, "Do you want to get into bed with Grandma?" Lola said, "No."

I smiled and said, "It's okay. Are you kind of scared?" Lola said, "Yeah."

She decided to look at some books, and visit with her mom and dad.

Louise gave me two-month-old baby, Emily putting her in my hands. I was amazed at how heavy the baby was.

Immediately, I said, "Oh, my gosh, Louise, you've gotta take Emily back. She's really heavy."

I was afraid I'd drop her. Louise quickly picked up Emily, and sat down next to me. I was frustrated that I could barely hold my own grandchild. I had to keep telling myself that I had had major heart surgery, and almost died. I had to give myself time to gain my strength back!

My sister, Paula, her husband, Dave, and their daughter, Lauren, came to see me on August 31. They came daily to stay with my husband and daughter, Rose. They also offered their hospitality of housing my husband, and assisting him with directions to the hospital, food, drink, and whatever else he may need after he made arrangements with whatever he needed to take care of in New Ulm.

I had forgotten how blessed I was with family and friends until this happened. I kept thinking the whole time that I still didn't know what I had done to deserve all this!

In the meantime, phrases to a song kept going through my mind about even the mountains bowing before the grandeur of God. I still didn't know what it meant, but I kept hearing those phrases. One more phrase came through about people shouting praise to the Lord.

The tune became very familiar to me, but I couldn't remember all the lyrics or the reason why I kept hearing it. I figured the meaning of the words would come to me at some point. I paid particular attention to the song to see if I could hear any more words.

More visitors had started coming on Saturday, and they shared their stories with me, although I hadn't shared my experience yet. I remembered my cousin, Marc, and his wife, Sandi, from Andover, Minnesota, came to see me. I was so glad they had come. I wanted to tell them that, but I couldn't. I tried shouting that I was okay, but they didn't hear me. I don't even think I knew what had happened to me yet.

Rod's Uncle Buddy and his daughter, Jody, came. I was exhausted at first, and asked them to wait. I napped for a while, and then felt bad about having them wait. I really appreciated their visit. Uncle Buddy was wearing an oxygen tank, so it was quite the challenge for him to come.

At some point, I remember our friends from Prior Lake coming. Kevin and his wife, Brenda, have been our friends our whole married life, and longer with Rod, since they were in high school together. I vaguely remember waking up and seeing him.

Rod said, "Jean, look who's here?" Kevin raised his hand and said, "Hi."

That's it. That's all I remember about Kevin's visit, and then I was out. Kevin, too, visited every day with Rod until I awoke, but I don't remember his visits.

Saturday night, Paula and Dave came back with Lauren. They brought a special surprise and grabbed a CD of old family pictures my sister Barb made one year for Mom and Dad's anniversary. Since none of us are too technically adept, we couldn't start the movie. We called for one of the nurses to see if she could help.

Finally, the right person came, but the movie Paula brought didn't run in the equipment the hospital had. Instead of watching the movie Paula brought, we watched *Rudy*, a great football story about Notre Dame.

I learned that my husband had heard of my emergency by answering the frantic pounding on our door. A police officer explained the situation, and Rod met me at the ER in the hospital about an hour before I was airlifted to Abbott in the Twin Cities.

Prior to his leaving the house, Rod had called our oldest daughter, Louise, who met him at the hospital in New Ulm. I didn't know Rod and Louise were at the New Ulm Medical Center.

Louise asked one of the doctors, "What happened? This is a healthy 52-year-old woman! Why can't you fix her up here and send her home?"

The doctor said, "No. Not with this issue."

The hospital staff at the New Ulm Medical Center was already taking the necessary steps to airlift me to Abbott when Louise and Rod even came. I have a sneaking suspicion the doctors in New Ulm had an idea of what I had, but couldn't diagnosis my condition, as they didn't really have any concrete results in yet from testing to confirm it.

Louise joined us in the Twin Cities the following day after making arrangements for her children. Our daughter, Rose, arrived at Abbott before Rod since she lived in the Twin Cities.

Rose answered the cardiologist's medical questions about a living will and other medical issues before the helicopter landed from New Ulm. She explained that I was neither DNI (Do Not Incubate) nor DNR (Do Not Resuscitate).

He gave her a look and said, "Does she have a living will?" Rose said, "No. She is full code."

The doctor asked, "Is this updated?" Rose said, "Yes."

Because my directives were current, doctors could do whatever they needed. Rose was there the whole time and in and out of my room constantly. She started praying, and put me on her church's prayer list. That became the start of my visitor and prayer list.

In a later conversation with Louise, I finally asked, "What happened to me in there (meaning the New Ulm Medical Center)?"

She gave me a quizzical look and said, "Don't you remember? You were awake the whole time."

"I was? Was I coherent?"

Louise said, "Yes. You know they shocked you twice." "No, I don't remember much in there."

I remembered one of the nurses told me I had a catheter, and one of them asked me if I had drunk any more than my family told them about. I hesitated with the alcohol question, because I wasn't sure what my family had told the doctors. Strangely enough, I felt like the nurse knew I did know how to answer. Then I shook my head in agreement with what my family told them to tell her something.

The only other thing I remembered was being lifted onto the

helicopter, and I was shocked in there. I knew bodies and minds were remarkable, but I found it really strange that I was coherent yet, had no memory of what had happened.

Our friends, Kevin and Brenda, came back on Sunday. By then, I felt pretty good. I was talkative, and was eating while the nursing staff prepared everything I needed to move to the fifth floor. YEAH! Almost time to go home. Kevin and Brenda stayed for quite a while, and left when the staff were preparing to move me. Yeah! Up to the fifth floor!

I enjoyed and appreciated all my company.

CHAPTER 6:

THE FIFTH FLOOR!

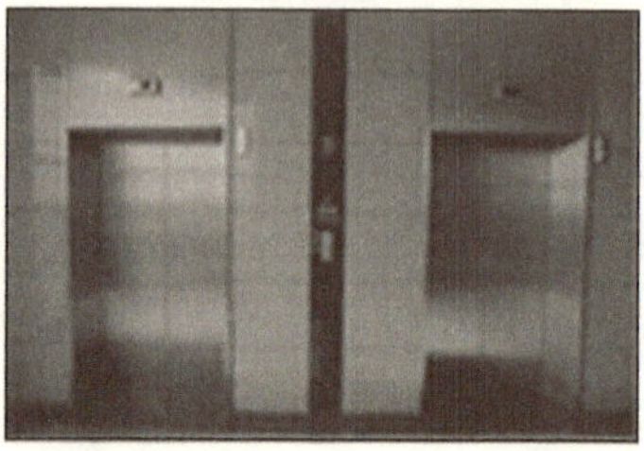

ON SUNDAY, SEPTEMBER 1, the cardiologist announced, "Jean, they have a room cleaned on the fifth floor now, and we can send you up there this afternoon!" That was quite a relief. Finally, I didn't have any more big tests to worry about, and even looking forward to a nice hot shower! After 6 days without a shower, that was going to be a treat! Plus, I knew I really was *out of the woods.*

Around 2:00 Sunday afternoon, I was moved to the fifth floor. Nurses Rosella, Justin, and Bruce assisted me. Rosella told me about the message from my physician. She said, "Do you know your physician from New Ulm wrote you a message?"

"No. What did she say?"

"Your physician says, 'We are so glad you're doing so well and are praying for you!'"

I smiled and said, "Yeah, that's her. She's fine to use the word prayer over the Internet."

Nurse Rosella laughed and said, "By the way, did you get your picture?"

I said, "No. What picture?"

Rosella said, "Hmm, let me look for it; it must be around here somewhere."

She came back with a picture of my heart, which tells me what I had, and what Dr. Henry did. It was really intriguing. Rosella amazed me with all the computer technology, because she was older. She was proud of showing up the younger nurses, and that she had found the message on the computer and the heart picture that went with it. Nobody else even thought about finding the picture for me. She made sure they all knew that, too. Good for her! Thank you, Nurse Rosella! It's important for people to have this information. The patients want to remember and know everything that happened.

I was fascinated, learning about the advantages of the computer, and my condition: SCAD: Spontaneous Coronary Artery Dissection. Nurse Rosella told me her girlfriend had a heart condition similar to mine, and that her friend had made a full recovery. She was quite encouraging, and I found it refreshing to have someone near my age helping me.

Before Nurse Rosella left, some good friends of ours from New Ulm came. We met Jill and Mark through Rod's work. Their daughter, April, came with her boyfriend and son. They brought gorgeous flowers for me. Nurse Rosella let them in, and said they couldn't stay too long, because I needed my rest if I wanted to get out of there.

April, an LPN, filled me in on one of the things that had happened to me at Abbott, of which I had no memory. She said that it was pretty common that I had pulled out the breathing tube.

Jill said everyone at work was surprised that the heart attack patient was me, and they were all praying which meant more prayers from a group of people were being said.

When I told Jill the whole story (not my visit with God yet— only about the ER trip), she was amazed how well my body reacted to such a rare and unpredictable condition. She got teary-eyed and even said, "Scary."

That first afternoon on the fifth floor, Dad walked in the room and said, "Look at you. You're a M-I-R-A-C-L-E!" I love how he drew out that word! Mom came in behind him, and we hugged and visited for quite a long time. I told Mom how I heard her voice when she was talking to the nurses, and how I had tried banging on the rails for her, but she wasn't aware of my efforts.

Then my sister, Barb, came. She told me she added my name on the schools' prayer chain. Barb was the principal of Catholic school in Bloomington, Minnesota! She also told me her children, Laura and David, prayed for me. Laura was in college in Wisconsin, and David was leaving that week.

Dad told me that when I was out, he went to see me and said, "Jean, it's your Dad!" He thought he could see me smile, but it was really quick. Neither Mom nor Dad seemed to want me to focus on too much on my predicament, as that was all they would tell me. They wanted me to focus on my wellness. After a couple of hours, they left.

Later that night, Rod's cousin's wife, Kris, called. She talked to me on the phone while Rod and Rose, were in my room. We talked a bit. Then she surprised me.

She asked, "So, did you have any out-of-body experiences when you were out?"

I was surprised she asked that and I said, "I don't know what this is." So… I told her my story. Then I said, "What do you think?"

She, in amazement, said, "Wow." And then she was silent. That was the first hint of my experience coming out.

After Kris fell silent, I was hesitant to pursue the conversation and thought, Oh, oh, maybe I should've kept my mouth shut. Well, it's too late now. The cat's out of the bag. I guess I'll just see what she thinks.

I knew she considered life-after-life stories true, and I don't know why I thought that, but I felt like she'd understand. We dropped the conversation at that point.

That conversation with Kris was when my visit with God had a hint of coming out. I was concerned now, because I wasn't going to tell Rod or family about my experience. But since I told Kris about it, they heard it too. I thought, *Oh, well, they don't have to think it's real if they don't want to.* I felt relieved after telling my story. At least, she believed me! She wasn't sure herself as to what to call it. After Kris and I hung up, I needed to figure out what Rod and Rose thought. I can't remember who started the conversation, but I said to Rod and Rose, "What do you think?"

Rose said, "Wow, Mom. You should write that story down."

I was shocked at her response, because I never knew her to believe in such experiences.

Rod got wide-eyed and said, "Wow!"

I don't know if he knew quite what to think. But at least, neither of them thought I was a nut.

Rose said, "Were you down and looking up or were you up and looking down?"

I said, "I was down and looking up."

Then Rose said something like, "You weren't quite over." Because Rose said that, I knew for sure I was talking to God **and the experience was real!**

I didn't know what to call this experience. But I thought, *Oh, well, who cares? Thankfully, my family thinks it's real!* Now, I felt more excited about sharing it, and finding out what I should do with it. Little did I know how big this experience was going to become!

One fact about the fifth floor is it's very noisy. The nurses kept checking on me that Sunday night about every four hours. It also must be where the helicopter lands, as I smelled the fuel from those, which was horrible! Every time one of them came, I said lots of prayers for the person, family, and crew. I knew prayers worked for me, and the persons in the helicopter were in life threatening situations, and that's exactly why they needed prayers.

Monday was Labor Day. The dietitian came to talk to me about a low-salt diet to keep my blood pressure down and fluid away from my heart.

I said, "But I don't have high BP, see?"

She said, "I know, but it's a preventative measure now, because of the 7 stents you have." She added, I'd be going to cardio rehab, and someone from New Ulm would be calling me in a couple weeks.

Then she checked to see who it was. She came back and said, "Her name's Clarice, so you should be hearing from her soon." At that point, I thought I'd wait until she called. Actually, I wasn't 100 percent sure all this wouldn't end up lost in the shuffle of things, so I didn't dwell on cardio rehab.

On Tuesday, the official word from Nurse Ingrid that I was well enough to go home came! I was excited and nervous all at the same time. She asked me if I knew what time my family was coming.

I said, "I think around noon today."

She said, "That'll be fine. I'll prepare your discharge papers." She worked on that and I said, "I'll need a work slip."

She said she'd prepare that too.

I packed with Nurse Ingrid. Then I showered, and dressed in regular clothes. This was the first time I could tell I lost a lot of weight. As I prepared for my shower, I looked down, and saw how thin my legs were. It was scary seeing myself in that fragile of a condition. I had weighed 115 pounds going in to Abbott, and that morning I weighed 102 going home! I had lost 13 pounds in 8 days! That was a weird feeling. I hadn't realized how much of my physical self I could lose in such a short time.

Now, I waited for my ride home!

Today, I continued to thank God, praise God, and pray constantly to God for letting me go home without major health issues. All I had to do was cardio rehab, take my blood pressure four times a day, consume 10 pills a day, and watch my salt intake. That's nothing to endure. I'm fully aware that my life could have taken a worse turn. At any moment, the turn could be much worse!

So, that's it: ten pills! I'm a normal person with two arms, two legs, and a whole body that works! I thought to myself, That's not too bad. I can do this. I know a lot of people in more difficult circumstances than mine. I'm amazed!

All I went through and all I have now is because of all the prayers people said for me, whether they knew who they were praying for or not. God has given me another chance here on earth because of all those prayers, and I have a fairly healthy body! I was exhausted, excited, and nervous all at the same time. I was eager about going home, but puzzled.

I started thinking that people are miracles; all people. But somewhere along the line we seem to go out of our way to be hurtful, whether the hurt was physical or spiritual, to those miracles who walk among us. I couldn't understand the cruelty of it.

I felt like a miracle when all those prayers were being said for me, but I don't know why? I'm not rich or famous. I have no clout, no status, and no great accomplishments. I'm just an average Catholic-born-Wisconsin-native-German-Irish-Swiss-Luxembourger-Green Bay Packer fan! Yet, all those people were praying for me and calling me a miracle!

Chapter 7:

Going Home

On Tuesday, September 3, 2013, I called Rod around 10:00 that morning to let him know I could go home at any time. He was pretty excited.

Rod and Paula, came around noon. Abbott faxed my medication orders to the pharmacy in New Ulm, packed me up, and helped me to the car with Rod and Paula.

I felt strange to be in a vehicle with no call lights and only a cellphone to call for help. There were no doctors, nurses, or hospital sounds. Rod had turned on the radio (I can't remember what station but probably, an oldies one).

I thought lots of different things, what we would do if I needed help, and what we would do if we had an accident. I had to quiet myself or end up having a panic attack, and going back to the hospital.

We stopped at Paula's and ate a healthy lunch with a low-salt diet of sorts and had coffee. After about an hour, I wanted to go home to have some normalcy and familiarity.

This time in the car, I tried resting and thinking about going home to my own bed. I wasn't picky; any bed would do! We were trying to figure out where to put me. Our house has two flights of stairs.

I could go to bedroom in the basement which has a 3/4th bath or upstairs to the bedroom with a full bath.

I decided not to worry about where I was going to sleep and let Rod, and our neighbor, figure out what to do. I napped most of the way home. When we arrived home, our first challenge was finding a way into the house. We decided to go from the garage to the porch instead of up the front stairs, which I was supposed to avoid anyway.

I sat in the car and let Rod bring in everything! Then, he found some lawn chairs, and set a couple of them on the sidewalk, strategically located, so I could rest between walking from the garage to the house if I needed.

Once we were in the house, I discovered our neighbor, and a couple of his kids had already put a single bed for me in the basement. I didn't have to decide where to sleep anymore! Their son had gone to college, so they had an extra bed. They made my bed and set up a tray, so I could have a phone, meds, water, and whatever else I needed close to me.

These neighbors had been our go-to neighbors when we needed anything, and they were glad to help. This is New Ulm, Minnesota: people helping people.

Rod was going to try to sleep upstairs. The basement wasn't equipped for two people to sleep there yet, as we were in the process of remodeling when all this happened. It did have an egress window, 3/4th bath, laundry, a room for the kids to play, and a TV. It had cement walls, which we planned to change to drywall during our remodeling project.

The stairs had a door leading to the porch, so in case of an emergency, I had two ways out. The egress window was one way, and the stairs going up and out to the porch the other way. The basement was safe to sleep in temporarily, but only for one person at that point. Rod and I had decided to remodel, had supplies ordered and people hired to redo the entire basement, but we hadn't started it yet. Some supplies needed to be delivered.

Being discharged from the hospital stunned me, because I thought I had overcome my heart problems and could now do whatever I wanted. Well, I couldn't! Once I settled, I checked the instructions for my meds and contacted Walgreen's to see if they had them ready for me. Louise came over to help, bringing her baby with her.

Rod went to Walgreen's and purchased the necessary supplies, and over-the-counter meds. When he arrived at Walgreen's, they needed more time preparing the rest of my meds. He told the pharmacist our daughter, Louise, would pick them up later. Rod came back and started unpacking. Louise and I decided to check out the rest of the medical instructions.

After the long trip home, I was amazed at how tired I felt. After all, I only sat in the car for two hours. I didn't think that should be that exhausting. I became nervous looking at the medical instructions and trying to interpret them.

Walgreen's called and said the rest of my meds were ready. This was a perfect time for Louise to pick up my meds, since our youngest granddaughter was sleeping. I was glad the baby was sleeping. She was only two-months-old, so I didn't know her well. Besides, I figured if she was sleeping, what could happen, right? (You'd think by now I would quit asking that question.)

Well, she woke up and had a bowel movement. Rod was outside without a cellphone, of course. I thought I could do this. Unfortunately, I couldn't lift her because she was too heavy for me at her mere 10 pounds. I scrambled to change her, and finally finished, right there on the bed. I felt pretty proud of myself.

Thankfully, I demanded diapers, wipes, and a whole bottle for her before Louise left, in case! She was fussy after the diaper change, so I fed her downstairs. Instead of holding her, I laid her on the bed and fed her that way. I felt bad about that, since it certainly wasn't my preferred style of feeding a newborn, but it was all I could manage! I knew she'd be alright with it, and the main point was, thankfully, she was fed.

Louise finally came back with all the meds.

I said, "What took so long?"

She said, "They had to go over all of them with me before they'd let me go."

I said, "Oh, I didn't think about that."

I told her what her daughter had done while she was at the store. She laughed and said, "Well, it was good practice for you!"

I gave Louise a dirty look and said, "Hey that was tough; she's heavy!"

Louise and I started to organize my meds in the pill-planner caddies. Our granddaughter needed her Mom, so I tried organizing the meds myself. I thought I had done this hundreds of times for clients at work and thought dispensing my own meds should be easy. I didn't need any help. WRONG!

As I tried to sort my pills into the caddies, the effects of the trip developed. I became confused and tired. I had my pills before me, but mixed them up, as I was putting them in pill caddies. They looked too much the same: white and round.

Sure, each pill had a description or number, but reading those descriptions on the same-colored small pills was difficult. Louise even had a tough time reading the descriptions of what was on the pills. I became frustrated and scared.

While I looked at all those different pills, I became confused about instructions too. For instance, one prescription was written take one tab twice daily. With those instructions, I wasn't sure about specifics— such as times of the day, or any special instructions I was given at Abbott— such as which meds I was supposed to avoid if my blood pressure fell below 90, and which ones needed to be taken with food. Even though the instructions were very carefully explained to me before we left Abbott, they all of a sudden became very vague.

I started thinking about the severity of the consequences with such vague instructions. For example, I could have interpreted the instruction of taking a med two times a day, meaning take one tab at 8 a.m. and one at 10 a.m. This act could have been considered an overdose with the result, another trip right back into the hospital. All that extra chaos would result in a maddening waste of everyone's resources; time, effort and money; because of how I interpreted the instructions, which could have been taken care of from the beginning.

Technically, any medication error wouldn't have been mine or the pharmacy's fault. How would I have known if I had taken them at the wrong times, if the exact times weren't written? I had taken the pill twice a day as the instructions directed. And, since the specific times weren't listed, (or how far apart dosages should be) I had taken them correctly!

The pharmacy was also correct. They filled and had written the prescription, (take two times a day), as that was how they received it from the doctors. I knew doctors wanted my blood pressure to be low, but I don't think they wanted it low enough to put me in the hospital again. Can readers see how confusing interpreting instructions is? I'm confused reading this!

I should've waited to set up those meds until I was more alert. I learned a good lesson, and can understand how medication errors can happen anywhere when instructions are left too open-ended. After I had all that trouble as I tried to organize my own meds, I had realized how much people need to help doctors.

People could be proactive for their loved ones and themselves by asking doctors for more precise instructions on the prescriptions from the beginning. It's always good to ask! Doctors will gladly do this. They need to know the patients' preferences!

Walgreen's confirmed that practice, and said, that if doctors add specific instructions on the prescriptions' labels in the original prescriptions, then pharmacies could add those instructions to the labels from the beginning. Walgreen's emphasized that the specific instructions had to be on the original prescription labels from the doctor: not by the patient's request.

Gratefully, Louise finished feeding the baby, and I gave the medication instruction sheet to her to read. You would think reading those sheets between two college-educated people would be a cinch! Well, the instructions seemed too vague even to her! Since Louise wasn't there when we were at the hospital, she didn't know about the specific instructions, either- which ones the nurse was talking about to hold if my blood pressure was too low, or other specifics.

Finally, I said, "Louise, will you take them all back to Walgreen's and have them put the pills in the right bottles again? Maybe they can sort them out."

Louise said, "Sure, I'll take them back if you and Dad watch the baby."

We agreed, but this time I made Rod take a phone with him when he went out to do laundry in case I needed him.

Louise went to Walgreen's, and came back after about an hour. Louise said, "Okay, we figured them out."

Louise explained the instructions to me, and I was much more comfortable taking the meds. After that fiasco with meds, I was ready for a long nap.

After my nap, I decided to e-mail my friend, MaryKay. I met her when I started my job at HSI. As I said, I had known her for 10+ years, and I could talk to her about anything. I knew her response might take a couple days.

I wrote my e-mail, which was lengthy. It was my whole story about my visit with God and the fact that I didn't know if it was real or what I should do with it. To my surprise, MaryKay e-mailed me back sooner that I thought! I was excited to see what she thought.

MaryKay wrote that she felt so bad, of course, that I went through all this, but my visit with God was definitely a very real experience. To my great despair, she hadn't given my experience a specific name. She called it a spiritual experience though, not necessarily a Near-Death Experience. I thought hmm, spiritual experience, this must be a new term. *She added that she felt God wanted me to share it.* At least, she believed me!

The first night at home went well. I needed to go to the bathroom once. I had Rod put a folding lawn chair between where I was sleeping and the bathroom. Then, I could take a break halfway if I needed.

Using the bathroom for the first time required some preparation as I had to realize how badly I would need to use the bathroom. I didn't want to have any accidents. I grabbed the cordless phone and my nitro, and not wanting to bother Rod, who was all the way up on the top floor, tried to make the trip on my own.

I walked to the bathroom slowly and gingerly, and I made it after only one short break on the chair. I repeated the break process on the chair on the way back to bed.

Once I was back into bed, I prayed as hard as I could so I wouldn't need to go to the bathroom again. By the end of the first week at home, I was pretty confident about going to the bathroom without ending up too light-headed.

By the end of the first week at home, I felt ready to go up to my own room. I walked up the stairs slowly. Thankfully, we had hand rails on both sides of the stairway, so I had something to grab in case I started to fall. I always had the cordless phone with me, and knew where it was (still do).

On Wednesday, September 4, 2013, my son-in-law, Bruce, called and wanted to know how I was doing.

Bruce said, "Mom and dad want to stop by, and say hi." I said, "They don't have to do that."

Bruce said, "It's okay. They really want to. Before I could say no that's okay, Bruce said, I'll call them and let them know you're going to be home."

I said, "Okay."

Brian and Ronda came on their way home from a road construction site. It was nice to exchange hugs, and especially see more familiar people. They asked about my situation more, and I showed them nurse Rosella's picture she gave me of my heart. Brian and Ronda couldn't understand how I survived all this. Brian lost his dad,

Richard to a heart attack that was unexpected. His dad was in his early 50s, which is why they were so interested in mine.

After they left, I decided to start working one of my goals; to thank the community and the hospital for all their care, expertise, and especially prayers, and that God and I heard all your prayers, and they worked. But how?

CHAPTER 8:

PRAYERS/GIFTS AT HOME/HOSPITAL

As I DEBATED how to accomplish my two goals; thanking the community and medical center, and letting people know their prayers were heard by God and me, and they worked, while I was writing it, I thought, How *am I going to do this?*

I received more and more cards and gifts every day. I still didn't know what I had done to deserve all those prayers and gifts. I had to figure out a way to thank everyone, and let them know their prayers were heard but how?

From the time I was young, Mom and Dad always taught me the importance of writing a thank you to people who had sent gifts or money for special occasions. The importance of this practice was to show your appreciation, and a way to let people know you received the gift.

Mom and Dad said, "You didn't necessarily have to write a thank you for only a card, but definitely if I had received a gift or money."

Mom mentioned the idea to me that it would be nice to write more than a note to the thank you, but I didn't necessarily have to. The main purpose of the thank you was to show my appreciation for whatever monetary gift I was given. She taught me to always go the extra mile.

Mom taught me the consequences if I didn't write a thank you. The main consequence was that people might think I didn't appreciate their thoughtfulness and shouldn't necessarily expect another gift from them for other occasions. After all, writing a thankyou was a simple and appropriate way of thanking them for their time, effort, thought, and money.

I wanted to continue receiving gifts, so I always put that thank you lesson into practice. I frankly enjoyed writing thankyou notes, and would take Mom up on her idea, go further and wrote a letter. I figured if I was going to take the time to write a card, I might as well write a letter too; it was an easy task to do. I used this letter-writing idea for Christmas cards. I sent cards and handwritten letters with Christmas cards.

Interestingly, people always noticed the letter I had handwritten for Christmas cards, and made a big deal out of it, especially aunts and uncles. I didn't know why writing a letter with a Christmas card was such a big deal. After all, it was only a letter, and something I was supposed to do. The letter came with the Christmas card whether they wanted it or not: hee, hee! As I said, writing was fun for me.

Consequently, while I composed my thankyou letter about my experience, I had an idea on how to share it. I thought, I know. *I'll write the thank you for the community and the medical center and have it printed in the New Ulm Journal, which is the local newspaper.*

I called Louise, and she came over with our youngest grandchild to help me figure out what to do with this article for the paper. Louise read the rules on-line.

She said, "You can do two things with it; either put it in a section of the paper where they can edit it if they want; or put it in the Letter to the Editor column where they can't edit it.

I said, "What's the difference?"

Louise said, "The difference between the two areas is this: If you put an article in the Letter of the Editor column, you need to sign your name to the letter to verify the authenticity of the article (as that's a new rule now in New Ulm for publishing letters to the editor). In the other section of the paper, you don't necessarily have to sign your name to it, but the paper has the right to edit the article."

I wanted every word printed as I wrote it. Since I was afraid they might delete the word God, I said to Louise, "Okay, put it in the Letter to the Editor column. It really goes out to the medical center and the community, and I want every word included."

Louise typed, reread, and I signed my name electronically to authorize the Journal to print it. She pushed the key to submit the letter for print. Once an article was submitted, there was no turning back. It was a matter of time before it was printed. After shesubmitted it, a message came up that the Letter to the Editor was going to be published on Wednesday, September 18, 2013.

I was disappointed publishing my thank you for the New Ulm Medical Center and community was going to take that long. Ithought too much time would have gone by for people to care about what happened to me. I actually thought about forgetting the whole thing, but I figured oh well, my letter was still worth printing. It's never too late to write a thank you. The medical center and the community needed to hear what happened. Maybe then, the media would realize what a great medical center and community we had even though we are relatively small in New Ulm, Minnesota.

After I submitted my letter to the Editor for the Journal, one of my goals was done: thanking the medical center and the community. After I wrote the article for the paper, I wanted to work on the second part of my goal, to let everyone know that their prayers were heard by God and me, and they worked!

'Having completed the first part of my goal, another idea came to mind, as to how to complete the second part of my goal; to let everyone know their prayers were heard by God and me, and they worked. I decided to go further. Even though I was taught to only write a thank you to people who sent monetary gifts, I was going to write a thank you to those who sent cards and said prayers, too, and send a copy of my Visit with God to them. Their prayers were important and heard by God, and they were important to me, too. Even though it was only me, just an average Catholic-born, Wisconsin-native, German Swiss, Luxembourger, Green Bay Packer fan, I know I wouldn't be here without those prayers.

I realized that I didn't care what people called or thought about my experience, I wanted them to know their prayers were heard by God and me, and they worked. That was my focus; instead of naming my experience, my letter was to tell people their prayers were heard! I figured whoever received a letter could take whatever information out of it they wanted; the physical or the spiritual aspects of it, fine. They could decide.

I didn't care what they did with my letter, I knew the physical end was equally important as the spiritual end. Those receiving my letter needed to know that both aspects of a person were involved.

So that's it, hands down, I decided I'd send my Visit with God letter out with a thankyou for the gifts, prayers, and cards I received, too. That's how I was going to share my letter. After I figured that, I knew my goals were done. Again, I didn't care what my experience was called or what people thought of it, but the other part of my goal was done: sharing my visit with God that is! Done!

I finished writing my letter and gave it to Louise. She went home, typed it, and saved it into her computer, so she could print it out. When she finished, she called and said, "What do you want to call it?"

I thought, *Nothing. I'm having a tough time figuring out what to call it, whatever it is.* But then it dawned on me that she wouldn't know what I might be referring to. I was already struggling with the issue of what to call it but wanted a title for the letter.

I said, "How about *A Little Visit with God.*"

Louise didn't hear the word "Little" and titled my letter, *A Visit with God.* I wanted "Little" in the title because to me, my visit with God was just that: a little visit. It seemed like a very short visit. I didn't think when I was with God that I was with Him for such a long time: certainly not for two days! It was just a short visit!

I had Louise make about 10 copies. That's how many thankyous I was going to write at first: ten. The response turned out to be amazing! And so, sharing my story began. My Visit with God was BORN!

A Visit with God

One night at work I experienced severe heart symptoms. The result was being flown to a major heart hospital and having emergency heart surgery. The condition is called SCAD, a Spontaneous Coronary Artery Dissection. It's a rare disease targeting women between their 30s and 50s, often going through pregnancy or menopause. This major heart institute only gets 1-3 cases a year and 2-3 don't live. They were able to put 7 stents in and had me under for 2 days.

It was during this time I had a little visit with God. It was a strange place as I hadn't seen it before and looked around to realize I was alone. Gradually, I looked up toward the Heavens and saw some clouds approaching. Thinking it might be my time, I asked God if I could borrow a little bit more time because Lily and Eve need their Grandma Jean. God said, "well, what are you going to do for me?" I said: "I could still become a better person."

At this point God was still deciding what to do when suddenly voices were heard. They were mumbling quietly at first, as if off in the distance, but kept getting gradually louder and louder. I looked up at God and said: "Look, I think they're praying for me." God said: "Well, I guess I'll give you another chance." When I started to wake up, I could see a priest giving me the Anointing of the Sick. As I slowly became more alert, there were family and friends surrounding me, and doctors and nurses all telling me what a miracle it was I was still here.

As stories continue to be told to me of the whole experience, and the pieces begin to come together, my knowledge now is that the voices were people praying for me. It got louder and louder as more and more people found out about my condition. There were people praying from New Ulm, Red Lake Falls, Fosston, Bemidji, LaCrosse, the twin cities, all the way to my aunts in California and their whole order of sisters. There were just so many other areas, Arizona, Iowa, Illinois; and different religions all coming together to pray for the well-being of one person.

During this visit with God I told him I could still be a better person. Telling people this story is my way of doing this. My goal here is to get everyone to understand how important prayer is and that it works. I'm living proof!

Please know if you can do one thing for someone who is in grave need, prayer is the best gift you can give them. Imagine if we were all on our church's prayer chains, how many more prayers people would receive. One day, we could maybe achieve world peace! It may be a small gift to some but it makes a big difference.

Sincerely in Christ,

Love, Jean

The first group of people who received a copy of *My Visit with God*, of course, was my family. I sent a letter to Mom and Dad and all my sisters and brothers-in-law.

Then I sent a copy to our prayer chain coordinator. I knew she had me on the prayer chain list from Louise, so I sent one to her. In the written part of the thank you, I added for her to share with people she knew who said prayers for me, too. I knew I didn't know everyone who said prayers or was on the prayer chain list, but writing this permission to the thank you was at least a way of giving others permission of sharing my letter with more people.

I wanted everyone possible to know their prayers were heard by God and me, and those prayers worked! By writing this additional note, our prayer chain coordinator could send one to all the parishioners on the prayer chain. She sent a letter to them, and a get-well card to me.

The first person I heard from regarding *My Visit with God* from the church was Marion. She actually left a message on my voice mail and said, "Jean, this is Marion. I got your letter and want you to know that I thought it was so inspiring and heart-felt. I wanted to call and tell you about it."

I called her back right away and asked, "How did you get one as I didn't remember sending one to you specifically yet?"

Marion explained, "I got a copy from the parish prayer-chain coordinator because she had permission from you that it was okay for her to copy, and send one to everyone on the prayer chain. I talked to her about it, and we agreed that your letter gave us goosebumps from reading it. I was wondering if I could make copies, and send it to my family?"

I said, "Sure, if it helped, you can make as many copies as you want. I want people to know their prayers were heard, and that they worked! Do you really think my letter read okay?"

Marion said again, "It was so moving and inspiring that I got goosebumps."

I was relieved at this response, because one never knows how much people feel about those experiences.

After I heard Marion's request about wanting to make copies for her family, it generated that additional message in the thank you from then on, for others to copy and share my letter to anyone they knew, who said a prayer for me, but frankly anyone who wanted one whether they said a prayer for me or not. I wanted to emphasize how God heard their prayers, and that they worked!

During this conversation, Marion asked, "Have you ever read the book, *Proof of Heaven* by Eban Alexander?"

I said, "No, but I think I heard about those experiences."

Marion said, "I have the book, and thought you might like to read it. There was a chapter in it that was strange to read but this book might help explain what happened to you."

I said, "Sure! It'll give me something to do." We both laughed at this.

Then before I could offer a way to pick up the book, Marion said, "My husband and I will drop it off while running our errands."

She came with it the next day, and I was off and reading it. Marion later sent another card and Novena of Masses to be said for me too.

After my letter was written and sent, hundreds of calls came from it. Louise continued making copies of my Visit with God letter. I'd have her make copies in groups of ten, as I didn't want to have extra copies around. By the time all was said and done, hundreds of copies of my Visit with God were sent.

I believe so many people wanted copies because our prayer chain coordinator made copies with my permission to everyone on the prayer chain to share it with whomever. Those comments from our prayer chain coordinator made me continue to add permission for people to share the letter with anyone they wanted.

Louise finally decided that, because so many people wanted copies of my letter, instead of making a few copies at a time, she'd make several more copies at once! It was a nice feeling that so many people requested copies, and better yet, **YOU BELIEVED ME, YEAH, YOU REALLY BELIEVED ME!**

I felt such relief, especially, because I had never felt like I had any impact convincing adults of anything; yet, you were adults, and you believed me!

After I completed those two goals, I decided that's how I fulfilled my response to God of how I could still be a better person in order to have another chance of keeping my earthly body, by writing the Letter to the Editor in the paper, and sending a copy of my Visit With God letter to all those who sent gifts, and said prayers.

After my two goals were done, I could finally develop a life routine again. But, I needed to take care of my personal wellness.

CHAPTER 9:

WELLNESS

AFTER I FINISHED writing the article for the paper and sharing my story, I decided to make a few phone calls to developa life routine again. One was to the assisted living facility and the other was to Curves. I wanted the assisted living facility to know I still wanted to work there and knew there was a way to put a hold on your membership at Curves so I needed to call both places.

Well, the assisted living facility was first this week (September 3-6, 2013), and our nurse answered. She was so great to talk too on the phone. Nurse said, "We were all so surprised about what happened. I couldn't believe you had gone through that."

Me: "I never thought it was a heart issue as I never had heart problems. I think that's why I waited so long to call anybody. I thought it was only old-female issues."

Nurse: "Can I share this with the staff?"

Me: "SURE! Please tell them, thank you for covering for me.

Is the director in?"

Nurse: "She's on vacation but I'll relay the message to her when she comes back next week."

Me: "Okay that would be great. Thanks. I'll give her a call too."

Nurse: "You should take your time coming back and there was no hurry."

I thanked her again then hung up.

Again, this is New Ulm. How many employers would want an employee to come back after I created all this chaos on my first shift off training? They were willing to hold my shift for me, and let me take longer to heal if I needed.

Sure, some people might think the money for one shift isn't that much, what's the big deal? But hey, to me, one shift's pay is a lot of money. I was surprised the place of employment even wanted me back after all the trouble I caused. Again, how GREAT was that!

This week, too, I called Curves. I dialed and our manager, Carol answered! YEAH. I knew I could talk to her.

Me: "Did you hear I had a heart attack?"

Carol: "What? No! You! What happened?"

I told her my story and she couldn't believe it. She knew I didn't have any health issues to warrant any such health crisis happening, especially a heart attack!

Me: "Yeah, I'm wondering how to put my membership on hold."

Carol: "Yes, just ask your physician for a note, and then you don't have to pay out anything until you come back. Can I tell the other ladies what happened?"

Me: "Sure, I won't be able to say hi to them for a while. Plus, if they know, maybe they'll keep working out!"

Carol was the first person who said: "You know, Jean, working out here for all those years is probably a big reason why you survived!"

Me: "I wouldn't doubt it!"

Then, I thought I'll have to ask my physician about that comment Carol made when I see her.

Okay, those two phone calls were done. Whew! This week, I made, and received more calls to help develop a life routine. One call was an unexpected surprise.

The call was from the Cities. I recognized the number being from Abbott. The staff at the hospital said someone would be calling for a while to check on me until I was comfortable with what I'm doing with my meds and cardio rehab. I answered, and sure enough it was Abbott.

However, to my great surprise and pleasure, instead of this being a wellness check call, the call was from Dr. Tim Henry! I hesitated to respond, because frankly, I couldn't believe it was him, more so, that he'd take the time out of his busy schedule to check on me!

I said, "I'm so glad to hear from you! I was bummed that I never got to tell you thank you. Everyone kept telling me how you were leaving!"

Dr. Henry said, "I was so surprised they sent you home so soon! I had been gone for work that week, and left after I operated on you. I accepted a position, and was moving to a hospital in California as their chief in the cardiology department. When I came back, I wanted to check on you right away and they said, 'We sent her home!'"

I had a strong feeling now that I must have been pretty close to death but, again, nobody including Dr. Henry would still use the term dying. I also felt like I didn't want to come right out, and directly ask him if I was really that close to death. Frankly, I probably didn't really want to know the truth myself. There was another objective to his phone call too.

Dr. Henry's asked, "Do you know anything about Stem Cell Research?"

I said, "No, not really."

Dr. Henry, "With stem cell research, we inject stem cells into certain areas of the heart that were damaged so the heart pumps stronger. Because of the condition you had, and the area of the heart that was affected, you might qualify for one such study if you were interested in participating."

I said (wanting to do anything to stay alive), "Well, if it helps, but I don't know if my insurance company will cover any of it, and I should check that out first because otherwise we couldn't afford it."

Dr. Henry said, "Don't worry, the study covers the entire cost, so none of it will come out of your pockets."

I said, "Well, okay then," thinking it was the least I could do considering they saved my life and the fact that I didn't want to die!

Dr. Henry said, "I'll have one of my people call you." I said, "Okay, thanks for thinking of me."

Dr. Henry, once again, said, "I'm still so surprised they sent you went home so quickly!"

After we said goodbyes, I waited for this person to call, and thought about the last comment Dr. Henry said that, "I was so surprised they sent you home so quickly." I realized how close to death I truly was, because Dr. Henry reiterated that statement during the entire conversation.

I still wanted some verbal verification from the medical perspective about how close to death I was. Like I said, even Dr. Henry, who operated on me didn't use the term "dying or death". I didn't know what to think about how close to death I was.

I continued writing my thankyous for the gifts and cards I received. I wanted to make sure I remembered everyone, so started a written list of all the cards and gifts I received. I wanted to thank and remember what everyone had done for me.

Chapter 10:

Prayer List Home/Hospital

After I talked to Dr. Henry, I decided not to worry about how close to death I was. I focused on getting well and sent out more thankyous and copies of *My Visit with God.* I wanted to make sure, especially now after Dr. Henry's conversation, that everyone I knew who said a prayer for me received a copy.

(In the following part, I am uncertain as to the order this happened and who contacted whom! I've asked family to share their stories with me regarding this point but life continued. Here's a letter from Mom and Dad).

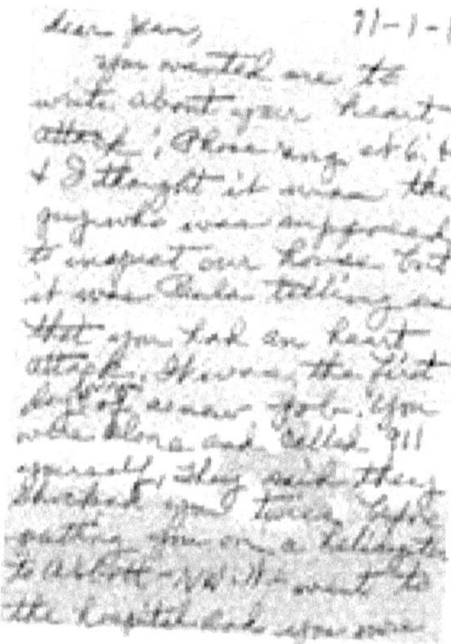

Dear Jean, 11-1-13
You wanted me to
write about your heart
attack. Phone rang at 6:45
& I thought it was the
guy who was supposed
to inspect our house but
it was [illegible] telling me
that you had an heart
attack. It was the first
day of a new job. You
were alone and called 911
yourself. They said they
shocked you 3 times before
putting you on a helicopter
to Abbott-NW. We went to
the hospital and you were

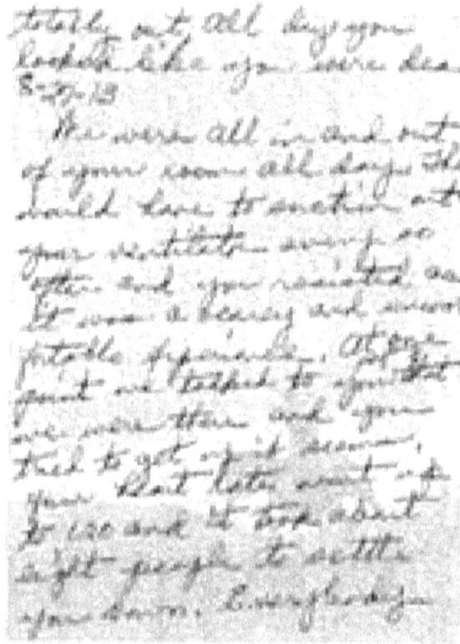

totally out. All day you
looked like you were dead.
8-27-13
We were all in and out
of your room all day. They
would have to suction out
your ventilator every so
often and you resisted as
it was a scary and uncomfortable
episode. At one
point we talked to you that
we were there and you
tried to get up it seemed.
Your heart rate went up
to 120 and it took about
eight people to settle
you down. Everybody

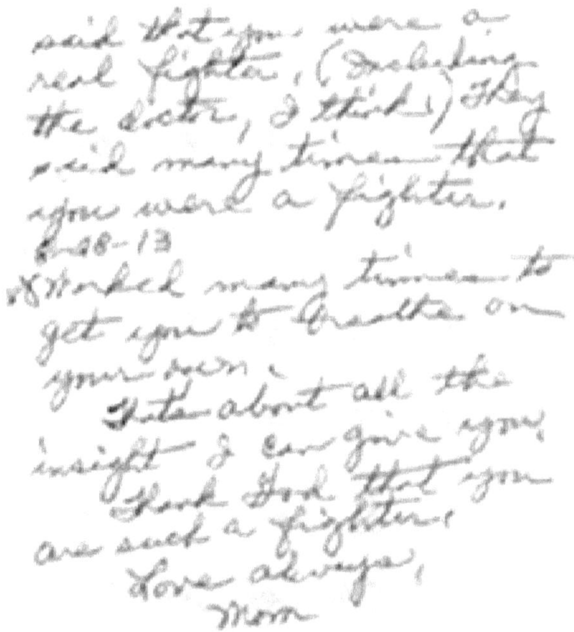

said that you were a
real fighter, (including
the doctor, I think) They
said many times that
you were a fighter.
8-28-13
I worked many times to
get you to breathe on
your own.
That's about all the
insight I can give you.
Thank God that you
are such a fighter.
Love always,
Mom

For me, hearing what happened when I was sedated is a way to always remember how much those prayers meant, and will always be remembered! So please, if a Near-Death Experience or serious illness happens to anyone you know, always tell your loved ones what happened. Even if it is difficult, sometimes unanswered questions from family members can be resolved!

Hearing others' stories also is a healing process. It makes those people feel like they are important, and that they mean something to somebody. It also fills in those gaps when the people were out. It's significant because the person learns that they were somewhere else, and where they were is different from where they are now. More importantly, they learn their experience was real!

My sister, Nancy had asked, "Do you know how many people were praying for you?"

I replied, "Maybe a few."

Nancy said, "You had hundreds of people praying for you, and clergy!"

I thought, huh! Why, it's just me. She must be kidding. I didn't think I even knew that many people!

Then Nancy told me about all the people she called to pray for me! Yes, between Nancy's comment, and by the time I finished my thankyous, I realized she was right! There were hundreds and hundreds of people who prayed for me! I couldn't believe it myself, HUNDREDS!

Nancy's comment about how many people prayed for me made that direct connection that the mumbling of voices from the silhouettes that came through, and the voices singing from above God and I saw and heard were definitely people, who prayed for me!

I was going to list them all here, but a very good friend told me to develop an appendix in the back of the book, and this will include everyone's cards, gifts and prayers said for me, so I did!

I thought I had all the people who said prayers for me accounted for after Nancy's comment. However, I was mistaken, again!

Chapter 11:

In the meantime-learning about more prayers Follow up Appointment

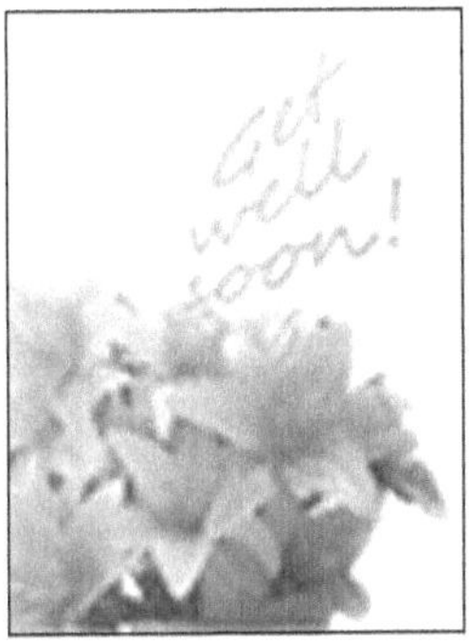

(September 9-13, 2013)

My next course of action, was to schedule an appointment with my primary physician in New Ulm. This was on Tuesday, September 10, 2013. Rod came with me, since I couldn't drive yet. At this appointment, I learned about more prayers that were being said for me from different groups of people.

The beauty of a parochial school is, of course, that students can pray! Somehow, Dr. Knowles found out about more prayers that were said for me.

Dr. Knowles said, "A class said petitions every day, and I heard your name was on the list because the class didn't know if you were going to make it."

Then she continued saying, "Usually, a prayer is on the list for a day with this class. However, the day the teacher found out it was you, and because of the seriousness of your condition, she decided to put you on for every day for the whole school year."

After I heard that the teacher put my name on her list of petitions for a whole year, I felt myself touched and cried over their kindness. That teacher had been in the Catholic school system for more than 20 years. She had taught our daughter, Rose!

I thought, What did I do to deserve all those prayers? After all, it was only me. I'm one person and haven't done anything really great per se. I'm just a Catholic-born-Wisconsin-native-German-Irish-Swiss- Luxembourger-Green Bay Packer fan! That's it, just a normal average everyday person trying to do good and serving God as best I could. I have neither clout nor status; yet, more and more prayers and now groups of prayers continued to be said, and heard by God and me! I am so amazed by all this.

Suddenly, like I made a connection with the silhouettes of the single heads that came through when I was with God after my sister, Nancy asked me if I knew how many people prayed for me, I made that same connection with the groups of silhouettes that came through after Dr. Knowles, told me about the classes, who said prayers for me.

After I made those connections of what the silhouettes meant, I knew the singing and mumbling of voices I heard when I was with God were really PRAYERS! I had told God— basically to save my skin— that I had thought those were prayers for me. WOW! They really were really prayers!

Now, since I heard that the students at the Catholic school prayed for me through petitions— and for a whole school year— my goal in thanking people grew! I wanted the students to know their prayers were heard by God, and that their prayers worked! I was also determined to find a way to thank the students, faculty, and staff for all their prayers too.

I wanted to especially thank the students so they understood how important prayer works, and how God heard them. By thanking them, maybe that would encourage the students to keep praying for others. Students' prayers are important too!

I also asked Dr. Knowles if my survival of the SCAD was because of regular exercise.

She said, "Absolutely! When you work out, your heart becomes stronger and can handle more issues."

I asked her, "Can I have a return to work note for Curves and work? One of the doctors at Abbott decided I could try and go back to work next week."

Knowing what I did for work, and realizing that soon of a return was impossible, Dr. Knowles said, "Well, we're going to change that. I don't like people going back until at least after cardio rehab."

She wrote a new return-to-work slip that would take effect after I finished cardio rehab— sometime after November— which made me feel better. I certainly wasn't ready to go back to work the following week, especially because of the strenuous work that I did!

I decided to ask Dr. Knowles about the Stem Cell Research which Dr. Henry wanted me to participate in. Dr. Knowles was from our church, and very much a practicing Catholic physician. I knew she'd be current on the church's teachings with this issue.

Dr. Knowles said, "It's always worth the time to check in on those studies. They can do amazing things with stem cells now. If at any time when you're there, you feel it isn't right for you then you can back out of it."

Because of her explanation and support of the research, I decided to go ahead and participate in the study.

My follow-up appointment was surprisingly quick. Rod and I actually asked my physician more about what happened that night (rather early morning) than what was going on with me now. We also talked about what Dr. Rayl and Dr. Henry did that night and how Dr. Knowles learned so quickly that I was there. Dr. Knowles explained that the New Ulm Medical Center and Abbott Northwestern Hospital were able to help me so quickly because of their computer systems.

Dr. Knowles said, "When patients go into the ER department, their physicians receive an e-mail with a red flag (or whatever it is). Then, the physicians can look it up to keep updated on all their patients no matter who they've seen or what happened. The Allina computer system is connected with other Allina hospitals throughout the state. When the New Ulm Medical Center ER department sent your information to Abbott, that's how they were ready to go so quickly when you arrived."

Patients are well-taken care of in New Ulm, Minnesota! At that point I thought, *Okay, there's some good with all this computer technology.*

Dr. Knowles continued with what happened that night.

She said, "Dr. Rayl was the attending physician. Evidently, he had a case similar to yours about a month before, and did the same thing. Since he happened to have a case so close to yours, that's how he knew what to do with you, and acted so quickly." (C'mon, the same doctor had this rare of a condition twice in a month in New Ulm, Minnesota. Nobody can tell me that was a coincidence! My case was only designed from God!)

The rest of the appointment was spent with routine tests. She listened to my heart and updated meds. We also scheduled upcoming appointments with my new cardiologist who gratefully comes to New Ulm. Yeah, I don't have to drag myself up to the Cities or so I thought!

After that appointment, I thought I'd send a letter to my physician. I wasn't sure how the medical center felt about spiritual issues. I didn't want to cause trouble by sending it, but I know she believed in prayer because she went to our church, so I thought she needed to have a copy. Besides, she said prayers for me, and mentioned the prayers coming from the school people.

I sent her a copy of *My Visit with God* letter.

I thought I had all the numbers of people, who prayed for me accounted for. At this follow up appointment, I learned about more groups of people and ages (children) who prayed for me. How rare is that? Learning about prayer at an appointment!

Rod and I went home. I napped, and slowly began to go through more mail, cards, gifts, bills, phone calls to employers, and whatever tidbits there were that were left to do. I continued to mail out *My Visit with God* thank you while still thinking, *What did I do to deserve all those prayers*

I thought all the prayers were accounted for after this appointment, but I was WRONG AGAIN! More and more prayers and gifts were forthcoming.

After I received all this goodness, I remembered lessons Mom and Dad taught me on how to always treat people with respect, kindness, and compassion because one never knows if what one said to a person would be the last words that person heard before he/she died!

CHAPTER 12:

WORDS OF WISDOM

ONE ACT I always hated from people was hearing them yelling, screaming, or fighting (even in sports, yes, even in football). Mom and Dad taught me that the only time I should yell for anything was when I needed help. They said people would respond faster if they knew when yelled, I needed help. Maybe that came from the social work side of Dad or from "The Boy Who Cried Wolf."

Mom and Dad taught me that when I had a conversation with anyone, I needed to consider how I would feel if the last words I heard from him/her was yelling and screaming. Since then, I always tried to put myself at the receiving end of a conversation. The result then would be that my words to that person would be positive, which was my goal, especially if those words were the last words a person heard from me.

Because of that lesson Mom and Dad taught me, I can't stand to hear someone screaming and yelling at someone else. After I heard about all those prayers that were said for me, I was glad I listened to

Mom and Dad's advice, and always tried to say something positive to the person to whom I was talking.

Walking home from church one day, I heard the following: "Jesus Fxxxing Martha, what the hell's the matter with you? Are you that gxdamn fxxxing stupid! I'm tired of bailing you out."

I had thought someone had a TV on, but I didn't care for that program. When I realized that was no TV program, I was appalled.

If I had heard those words, they would have made me feel like I was the source of all his trouble!

I remember those phrases like it happened yesterday. He repeated and repeated them: he didn't stop. I wondered what the heck the other person had done that was so bad that she deserved to hear those words.

Those words mean more now since my visit with God. They almost haunt me because I didn't do anything about them then, I ignored the situation. I thought, They're only words. It's no big deal. The person saying them didn't mean it. Besides, the person hearing them is on the phone, so nobody was hurting anyone.

After my visit with God— because I made a direct connection with the existence of God, Jesus, Heaven, and all the angels and saints— I know words aren't ***only*** words anymore. Even if he was on the phone, those words to the recipient were too direct. How do I know that person was truly safe!

Well, ***NEVER AGAIN*** will I believe any words that are said to anyone are only words or that words are no big deal, or ignore a situation like that. Now, I can't understand the cruelty of harsh words. If I can't stop the situation myself, I know to call the police, and let them handle the disturbance. They can do more to help than I can.

People in all areas of my life (work, neighbors, family) know how much I hate screaming and yelling that even individuals and staff at different sites, and fields realize it. I don't know how everyone knows this about me; it's not like I broadcast that to people, but it comes out somehow. Clients even know this.

My husband and I sometimes work with the same individual for our companies in separate areas of her/his life. One night, I worked with a client at her home, and Rod worked with her the next day at her job.

Evidently, she didn't like something I had done with her the previous night, when I had to take her shopping. So, she tried to ***bust*** me to Rod. She told Rod that I had yelled at her the night before! Rod was so taken aback by the comment that he stopped in his tracks and said, "Jean doesn't yell."

She looked up at him sheepishly and said, "I know." They both laughed.

Well, I told the team leader this story and she said, "Oh, it was probably because I told you she couldn't have something when you went shopping with her."

The team leader and I talked to the person the next week about the situation. Sure enough, the team leader was right. The individual was mad at me because I didn't buy her something since it wasn't on the list. The team leader admitted to the client the direction came from the team leader; not Jean, so she had no choice but to follow it.

However, the team leader also told her to make sure she is more specific, so we can grant her requests better, instead of her being sneaky about it! She laughed and said, "Okay, I'll try to tell you what I need more."

Notice the difference in the above experience of how a tough situation was handled that turned out to be good. We chose to handle the situation in a way that everyone benefited; the individual told us what happened, and we cleared the situation up without screaming or yelling at each other. The best part about that situation coming out positively was we all laughed in the end.

This is how one act of a behavior affected people individually, POSITIVELY! We all felt better about what to do in the future.

At the time of writing this, that person I had the issues with has died and gone to her Heavenly home. I'm glad we cleared up the situation up the way we did: positively! I'm glad she didn't have to justify what I had done to her about that shopping situation to God, but some people aren't so lucky! They don't have another chance to change words they might have told someone before they died.

After I realized how many people prayed for me, I wondered how people could say and do such horrible things to each other. That doesn't make any sense to me.

Well, as much as I hate screaming and yelling, I want to YELL at people now that GOD AND HEAVEN EXIST! STOP THE YELLING AND ARGUING! STOP IT! Negative behavior bothers me so much more because I know firsthand those truly could be the last words said to or heard by a person before he or she dies. Words people said are important.

After I was home for a while, I thought more about how I could fulfill my response to God's question that I could still be a better person and what more could I do about all of this to make a positive difference. I was overwhelmed at how much good people can do when prayer was involved. It's just me, a simple, Catholic-born, Wisconsin-native, German, Irish, Swiss, Luxembourgian, Green-Bay Packer fan! Certainly, I had no "clout". Yes, what can I do about this Near-Death Experience I had?

I wasn't going to fulfill my response I gave to God that I could still be a better person by sitting at home. I needed to do more. When I could be out and about more in the community, then I would have a better idea of what this "more" was that I was going to do.

I knew one thing for sure: instead of allowing people to scream, yell, or hurt each other, if I had a chance, I was going to stop them from saying horrible words! I realized I'd much rather have the last words anyone heard from me be POSITIVE, because gratefully, I had experienced that. I was blessed that the last words I heard before I left for work that night from Rod were, "I love you."

Next, I had to take care of another area of my life, so I could do something more positive about all of this! The one area of my life I started with is my personal life area. Rod and I decided to start slowly here since I was still home. First, I needed to have my life routine established.

CHAPTER 13:

(IMPORTANT FIRSTS)

First Outing

ZICKE! ZACKE! ZICKE! ZACKE! HOI! HOI! HOI! I don't know what that means, but saying it is fun, especially after a few beers! One of New Ulm's many fests was coming up, and that seemed like a good time to get back into the swing of things with my personal life. The first outing takes some planning. This outing wasn't too difficult or far, but it started the ball rolling and was still a first!

The outing was on our front steps. This was far enough as I was still weak, and hadn't gone too far (just to the clinic, a couple blocks away).

New Ulm is well-known for its variety of fests for every season and occasion imaginable. Hermann the German Days are held in early September. It's a celebration of our Hermann the German monument, a symbol of freedom. More importantly, the celebration is a remembrance of the Germans who founded New Ulm in 1858.

Rod said, "Maybe we should watch the fireworks outside."

Rod invited the neighbors. They set up a lawn chair for me to watch the fireworks. Rod helped me down the stairs. I was nervous, and didn't think the lawn chair was sturdy enough for me, so I sat at the bottom of the stairs.

The bottom of the stairs was far enough for my first excursion. I didn't want to go too far yet. I wanted to be close to home in case I had another SCAD. I thought I'd sit at the bottom of the steps with my coffee. Here I was drinking coffee, instead of beer and salt!

The night was gorgeous, and the kids thoroughly enjoyed watching the fireworks. Sometimes, I relate much better with kids than adults. As a matter of fact, most of the time, I relate better with kids. I believe this comes partly from my early childhood education, and since they're young yet, I figure I still have a chance to work with them. Hee! Hee!

Everyone tried to distract me because of my SCAD, by having general conversations about the fireworks, etc. We chose our home, because I needed recuperating, but also that was the best place to see the fireworks. This outing was a great way of seeing people I hadn't connected with yet and to remember I was back on earth.

Terry, our next-door neighbor, came out and sat next to me. I confessed to her that this was my first outing. She said, "I know because I had been watching, and I didn't want to come over until I saw you out. That's how I knew you were up to some company."

I laughed and said, "Oh, you could come over anytime. Plus, I'd really enjoy the company," and at this point, the security of having someone else with me.

I asked her, "How did you find out?"

Terry said, "I noticed you weren't around for a few days. I knew you were going to go up north, but I felt like it was something else because I knew you weren't going to go up north until later. Finally, I saw Rod outside, and asked him if you were on vacation.'"

Rod said, "No. She had a heart attack," and told me the rest of the story.

I felt bad Terry hadn't heard about my heart attack until then, because she's a great neighbor, but she understood.

That's our neighborhood, though. The bond with neighbors developed from the National Night Out parties we had. We know everyone on the whole block.

The best part of knowing the neighbors is that we all keep in touch with each other, especially the older neighbors. Even if we didn't know each other personally, we know who everyone is, and the kids know they could go to anyone if they need help.

During the end of the fireworks, a couple walked by, and the gal waved to me. I didn't recognize her but I didn't want to be rude, so I waved back.

Rod said, "Isn't that the gal you work with at the assisted living facility?"

I said, "Oh yeah!"

I called her name but she didn't hear me. My voice was still weak after I pulled out my breathing tube, so it didn't surprise me that she didn't hear me. I thought, *Well, at least she knows I'm fine and hopefully that I'll be back to work soon.*

After the fireworks were over, we went inside since the mosquitoes were coming out!

Hermann the German Days were a nice way of slowly developing a personal life routine. After this successful excursion, I decided to try one new activity every week. I knew I couldn't stay inside the house forever.

Plus, I wasn't going to allow fear to control me from serving others and God! I certainly wouldn't "become a better person that way", which is what I promised God in order to keep my earthly body.

A life routine was only going to happen with the help of the cardio rehab team. The next week, Monday, September 16, 2013, I received a phone call from Clarice at the New Ulm Medical Center. She had some openings and was ready to schedule an initial visit.

I prayed the team would skip the whole cardio rehab treatment. But no, of course not. They remembered, and the next sequence of life events started to unfold! After I checked with Louise to see when she could take me to cardio rehab, we set up the initial visit for the next Friday, September 20, 2013 at 1:00 p.m.

Yep, just when I thought my goals were done, writing the thank you in the paper and sharing *My Visit with God*, more goals developed: goals that neither others nor I had foreseen.

Now, one more area was taken care of: my first event from my personal life was done. The next area of my life that needed to be taken care of to help build a life routine was my physical area. This area could only be taken care of with help.

CHAPTER 14:

CARDIO REHAB

FRIDAY, SEPTEMBER 20, 2013— I was at the cardio rehab center in the New Ulm Medical Center with Louise and our granddaughter. I answered the questions Clarice, the head nurse, had for me. Then she told me about the program.

Clarice, explained, “There are five staff who take turns coming. There’s one nurse and one athletic trainer each session. You come for three (3) visits a week for about an hour each visit for two months. I thought, *Geez! That much time? I thought rehab was going to be one or two times, and they’d check me out.*

Clarice gave me my choice of times. We picked Monday, Wednesday, and Friday at 10:00 a.m. We knew Louise was going to have to drive me for the first couple times, so that time worked the best.

My first visit was on Wednesday, September 11, 2013.

Deb was the nurse and Tim was the athletic trainer. They reviewed with me how the program worked, and how it helped my heart pump stronger. I haven’t a clue what they were talking about, but figured I’d cooperate, because I didn’t have the strength or knowledge to argue with them. I only wanted to find out what to do about my own concerns and go home.

My primary health concern was being so tired. I talked to Deb about this.

She sat down and said, "Your body has to adjust to three things: the meds, the heart attack itself, and the stents."

I thought, *Ha, I don't want to adjust to any of this!* But I kept my mouth shut, not wanting to offend anyone. After all, it isn't her fault any of this happened! She continued with the overview of the rest of the program.

After the verbal instructions, the actual workout portion of the program started. My initial vital signs were taken which included my blood pressure, weight, and pulse, and then I started on the treadmill. As at Abbott, they found out I weighed only 102 pounds. Then they gave me this wonderful monitor to wear around my neck. It's really quite heavy since I was only 102 pounds.

After a few minutes on the treadmill, the staff showed me this chart and asked, "How hard do you think you are working?" The chart had a progression of five stages, which varied from very light to very difficult. I answered by choosing one of those stages.

They explained, "We need to know this because if you work out too hard, then you would need to sit and rest. You worked out oneach machine for twenty minutes."

I continued with this rehab routine each time I went. At the end of the cardio rehab session, I sat for about ten minutes. They measured my blood pressure again to make sure it was okay before they sent me home. This routine was what I endured for the next six weeks. As I improved on the machines, weight training was added.

Along with cardio rehab, I met more professionals. Those professionals provided me with information I needed to stay well.

First was the dietitian, who in the process of the conversation, discovered we knew each other from church. She reviewed my blood work, blood pressure, and she was confused as to why I needed a low salt/cholesterol diet. She asked Clarice about it, who verified that the low-salt diet was preventive basically because of the stents, and condition I had. "Doctors don't want to see her stents become blocked or fluid build around her heart, which is why the diets were important." After the dietitian heard Clarice's explanation, she continued with giving me the instructions I needed to follow with the low-salt diet. Then, she wanted to hear my story.

After the dietitian heard my story, she said, "God must have something 'great' in mind for you."

The dietitian taught me how to count the milligrams of salt intake, and handed me a booklet from the American Heart Association. This booklet explained, too, why I needed to stay under 2,300 mg of salt per day, and which foods were recommended.

Now, I challenge myself to see if I can stay under 1,000 mg of salt a day. It's a pretty easy challenge if I put my mind to it. I only have to read the labels, and make it a point to count the milligrams. After all, I know I'm here for our grandchildren, so have something to work towards.

The added incentive of staying under 1,000 mg of salt was that I DID NOT want to go back to either hospital until I was around 90! At that point, I'd do anything to stay alive!

The dietitian said, "Basically, if you stayed under 600 mg of salt per meal, you'd be okay without stressing about counting the salt too much. You can't get rid of all of it, but the 600 milligrams was a good amount to stick with per meal."

She ended the conversation by telling me, "Call me any time for anything." I thanked her for her help, and continued with the workout.

The next professional I visited with was the pharmacist.

After she heard my story, she too said, "You are here to do something great."

She reviewed my med list, and explained what my meds were for, and asked if I had any questions. I didn't have any questions, but told her what happened after I came home from the hospital about the confusion and issues Louise and I had while trying to organize my meds.

I mentioned that maybe physicians could add those specifics to the prescriptions right away, because patients feel like a bother when they ask. By adding directions on the prescriptions in the beginning, then, pharmacies can put those directions right on the prescriptions.

The pharmacist said she thought that was a good idea for the doctors to add those specifics to the prescription instructions right away. To date, I'm not sure if anything happened with the medical center doing anything about adding specifics to patients' prescriptions, but at least she was going to do something.

The pharmacist also told me, "If you have any questions, call any time."

After I met with those two professionals, the cardio rehab visits continued as maintenance as far as I was concerned.

I didn't see any benefits to those professionals or cardio rehab. I only worked out at the cardio rehab center, because I was supposed to. At the same time as cardio rehab, other life events had started to unfold. I thought my life was going to come together one step at a time. However, I was bombarded with more events that happened, and more than I planned!

Chapter 15:

More Life Events

During the week of September 16-20, 2013, nobody had contacted me about the research study from Abbott. I became concerned, and thought maybe I had the wrong information. I wanted to do my part for the research team before I returned to work. I knew once I returned to work, I wouldn't have any time off left in which to participate. My time to help Abbott with this research was running out.

I decided to call Abbott about the research. Amazingly, instead of hearing from an answering machine, I talked to one of the nurses. I told her my story about the ER trip, surgery, and how I had seven stents implanted.

I talked to the nurse about the phone call I received from Dr. Henry. I said that Dr. Henry was going to have somebody call me from his research team, but that hadn't been done yet. I wanted to know what to do about it.

She said, "Dr. Henry was moving out to California, but Dr. Traverse would be the cardiologist, who would perform the proc edure." This nurse reiterated to me, that she was amazed I had seven stents.

She kept saying, "Seven stents! That's unheard of!" Obviously, this SCAD is a life threatening condition that doctors truly don't know a lot about.

I don't know who's responsible for naming the term forNear-Death Experiences, but, **for me**, a life-threatening and/or unexpected rare health situation seemed to be the criteria to justify calling accounts concerning Heaven as a Near-Death Experience.

Since Dr. Henry's nurse was so emphatic about the fact that I had seven stents, I finally had enough nerve and asked her, "What made Dr. Henry keep going on me?"

She explained, "Dr. Henry is quite tenacious, and doesn't give up easily. It looked like he had trouble getting in with the angioplasty, and when he did, he chose the right spot and kept going."

The nurse spoke very cautiously while she told me what Dr. Henry did. I could tell because she spoke very slowly and deliberately. She probably didn't want to scare me, and like all the cardiologists did when I was in the hospital, seemed to avoid using the word dying. I suppose, technically, it wasn't her position to diagnose my condition.

The nurse connected me to Dr. Henry's Research clinician line. I left my name and number for them. I thought, *Well, by doing that, at least I'm trying to help. That is the least I can do for someone who saved my life!* While that was in the works more events happened as well.

This same week (September 16-20, 2013), my thankyou in the Letter to the Editor column appeared. This letter generated more positive results than I expected. But that's what my goal was: to produce positive results for the center and the community. As scheduled, my thankyou came out, Wednesday, September, 18, 2013.

Letter of thanks from me to Comm\ER\Staff for all their work. Put it in the Letter to the Editor section

Letters

Lucky to be living in New Ulm

To the editor:

The letter sounded great. It was weird seeing my name in print actually. One of the few times my name was in The Journal! Okay, it was self-initiated, but it was positive. Even though I had it printed in the section where they couldn't delete any words, I was thankful they didn't edit anything out of it, especially, the word God.

The only disappointing factor was The Journal spelled Abbott with only one t instead of two. Louise and I both questioned this spelling error, as we knew we spelled Abbott with two ts. But we know computers have their own quirks; figured it was a fluke, so didn'tmake a big deal out of it.

I didn't expect much from the letter. I wanted to do something good for the center. Hopefully, that letter would make the media more aware that small communities and hospitals do good work, too! Stories don't have to come from bigger hospitals all the time in order for them to be good. My letter produced positive results, which is what I wanted: positive results!

The first person from the community to notice the letter was our co-worker at HSI. She's always informed on current events going on in New Ulm, and world wide. This staff talked to our neighbors, and they added me on the prayer chain at Cathedral.

This coworker called right away and said, "Your letter was so nice and so good to hear."

Carol emphasized, "My roommate and I were doing our own research on how big your condition was. We, as well as the staff at the house, were all so shocked that it was you who went in [for a heart attack]."

Then she said, "If you need anything, let me know."

I thanked her for that offer, and I was surprised the article affected her that way, as well as my situation.

In the back of my mind, I wondered if I should share *My Visit with God* story with her.

The staff mentioned, "Our team leader put out the Paid Time Off (PTO) request for you, and I saw it. I don't have any PTO coming, but I want to send a gift of money and hope that will help."

The gift was greatly appreciated! The gift covered a lot of trips up to Abbott! Guess what? She received a thankyou, and a letter too. She was appreciative of both.

The same day my letter came out. another coworker, who recently returned from a leave herself, called. Dixie said, "It was such a shock… just a shock when I heard you went in with a heart attack! If you need anything, you call me. I'll help clean or wash floors, whatever you need."

It was so good to hear she was doing so well.

We had to laugh about our poor team leader having to deal with all our illnesses! Since May, someone was out every six weeks with unexpected conditions, until I returned in October much earlier than anticipated. All those unexpected conditions were spooky, and all for different reasons.

Dixie left the company that fall. I sent her a good luck card with a gift and letter too.

She said, "The gift and letter made her cry."

The day after my letter came out, more calls were slowly coming in about it. One call was from an unexpected person. The Marketing and Communications Specialist person from the New Ulm Medical Center called. She introduced herself as Kitty. She asked for my permission to print it in an Allina publication of sorts.

Kitty said, "It's a great story, and I was so appreciative of seeing it." Here, I had to laugh at myself, because to me it was only a thank you.

Plus, I didn't even know a hospital had such a thing: a PR department! Geez!

I said, "Sure, if it helps, you can PR that letter however you want!" I wanted everyone to know that the New Ulm Medical Center's Doctors DO **KNOW WHAT THEY'RE DOING**, whether anyone else thinks they do or not.

There was another point to Kitty's conversation.

Kitty asked, "Could the hospital print it in a publication Allina has with the Journal? It's the Health Edition of the local paper, which comes out every two months. That section tells stories such as yours, and the section is associated with the New Ulm Medical Center and the Heart of New Ulm Project." It's amazing what a little thankyou can do. Yep, even in this day and age a thankyou goes a long way.

I had no idea really what Kitty was talking about with that publication story, but I wanted to help. I said, "Sure! If you can use it, go ahead! Do you need me to sign something?"

I felt like people needed to hear this side of the story too: primarily the good side— the millions of good things that are done daily even at smaller centers and left unnoticed!

Kitty said, "Yes, you needed to sign a permission form, but I was wondering if I could take a picture of you, too. Maybe with your family. I could come to your house if you want me too."

I said, "Well, I'm actually at cardio rehab M/W/F at 10:00 if you want to come there instead, and that would save you a trip."

Kitty said, "Sure, we can take a picture of you on one of those machines."

I said, "Okay! You can use my story however you want to!"

I asked Kitty if there was some way to talk to Dr. Rayl about what he had done, since Abbott raved so much about how the New Ulm Medical Center had prepared me. She was going to check into it, and see what she'd find out anyway. We set a date on a Friday and she was going to contact Clarice for permission to come to cardio rehab and take pictures.

I told Kitty, "Thank you for thinking of me," and we said our goodbyes. Then more events suddenly evolved.

This week, too (September 16-20, 2013), Dr. Henry's nurse, Jane Fox called. We set up a time to go through the tests for this study. I requested a quick process as I had to go back to work soon. She was very accommodating and understanding. The only requirement for a date was that the infusion had to take place a month after the heart attack.

Jane and I set the date for the screening tests and the infusion was to take place the following week. When she told me the date of the screening, I said, "Oh, that's the day after my birthday!" Jane laughed and said, "Oh, it is?"

After I explained to Jane about driving restrictions, she assisted me with transportation, and hotel arrangements for the screening with all costs taken care of by the research study.

Jane also mentioned a packet of information would be coming in a couple days that told me exactly what was going to happen. A couple days later, as promised, I received that packet with information on Dr. Henry's work and a note saying I would be enthusiastically thanked.

I wasn't sure what Jane meant by that note, but thought, oh well, it's a nice thank you.

That was quite the packet of information! Jane sent me a couple of e-mails with the time frame of the tests, so that I would know what to expect that day. The information was a lot to absorb, since I wasn't familiar with stem cell research at all. I learned, too, that I would be the last recipient in this phase of the study, which was called the safety phase. This meant instead of receiving the placebos, I would be assured of receiving actual stem cells.

I was interested learning about stem cell research. I heard on a Catholic television network that the Catholic Church was not in favor of stem cell research. I wish I would have paid more attention as to why. I can understand some of the why the church wasn't supportive of stem cell research as God has the final call in our lives so really what good are stem cells.

But, with the circumstances that surrounded my story, I thought wow! God must want me to receive those stem cells. Maybe, if I received those stem cells, it was a way to tell the Catholic Church the procedure was fine. Plus, my own physician, Dr. Frannie Knowles, a very strong practicing Catholic, was supportive of this particular research.

Paula, was going to meet me at Abbott, but I had no idea how to tell her where to find me. My family was into a somewhat normal routine here. I didn't feel like asking them to take off any more work, and I wanted to give them a break.

I decided to take the van, which was a better decision than staying up in the hotel Jane mentioned, because I could come back home the same day. After I mentioned to Jane that I was taking the van, she said the cost of the van service would be covered by the study, and she canceled the hotel reservation.

During that week (September, 23-27, 2013), at cardio rehab, I started to build up enough strength and worked up to around two to three Metabolic Equivalent of Task (METs). The cardio team wants people at five METs by the time they're finished. The best part of being at five METs was I earned a prize! We're all thinking it must be a big prize, and worked hard to earn it. Building up to five METs was definitely a challenge, but the motivation of the prize helped. I won a pedometer, which I greatly appreciated!

During this week, my thankyou must've come out in whatever publication it was Kitty mentioned. At a cardio rehab session, Clarice said, "Jean, I read your thankyou in the section with the Allina publication column of how appreciative you were. Kitty sent your thankyou from this publication to the whole center, and I thought it was so nice."

I really didn't know what Clarice was talking about with this publication business with my thank you being sent throughout the whole center, but I said, "Thank you! I just hope it helps!"

Monday, September 23, 2013, I told Clarice, I'd be gone on Wednesday, the 25th to participate in this stem cell research study at Abbott. She was quite supportive of it, too. She checked me off the list for the morning at cardio rehab.

The cardio team said in the beginning to let them know whenever I would be gone, so they wouldn't worry. If I were gone without letting them know, they'd start to call to make sure I was okay.

In a way, the break from cardio rehab was going to be nice. I thought the break might give me a chance to reflect about the question God gave me when I was with Him. By participating in this study, I thought maybe something good would come out of it. At least, I'd be able to pray about why I had this Near-Death Experience, as people kept calling it.

More importantly than reflecting on God's question, "What are you going to do for Me," was the possibility that I'd discover an answer to my response: "That I could still be a better person." I didn't know what would happen by participating in that study, but whatever happened, prayerfully, *(as I thought the same thing when I was descending into Minneapolis about the works that I had done),* the result would be something good.

Chapter 16:

Stem Cell Research Part 1

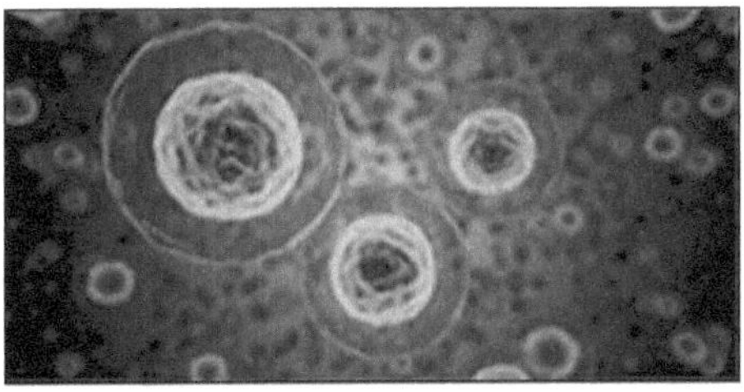

Wednesday, September 25th, 2013— We were off and running for Abbott around 6:30 am. There was one other passenger with me, and thankfully, I knew the driver. He didn't remember me, but I mentioned his wife's name as she was a Curves member with me.

As we drove to the Cities, I started to question my act of sending out *My Visit with God* letter, and I wondered if I had done the right thing. Interestingly enough, God reminded me that sending out *My Visit with God* was okay, and I was supposed to keep telling people my story. God told me this through others; people from the parish, my family, and our TEC family. They still sent me cards, gifts, and phone calls, and asked how I was doing.

One of those gifts was a book. It was the start of a couple books I was given on Near-Death Experiences. The first book I received about Near-Death Experiences was from Marion, the parishioner who calls me on the prayer chain. Marion gave me her book called Proof of Heaven, written by Eben Alexander about his Near-Death Experience (NDE) as he referred to it. She gave me this book because she believed that's what I had, a Near-Death Experience. I had barely begun to read this before the study.

Interestingly, I brought the book with to have something to do. I noticed the other passenger had a book. I thought, she must be expecting a long trip. I didn't know her at all, but we visited. I was in the middle seat of the van, and she was in the front. She had knee issues, so sitting up in the front was easier for her.

The noise of the van made it difficult for me to hear the conversation even with hearing aids. So, I didn't participate in it. I didn't mind, as I was deep in thought. I was also trying to forget how hungry I was because I couldn't eat anything until after my tests.

We finally arrived in the Cities. I wondered how I was ever going to find my way up to the second floor, let alone figure out where to go from there. I should've known that the New Ulm Medical Center's driver would worry about that for me.

The driver obviously had taken this trip many times. He parked, offered his assistance by taking my arm, found a wheel chair, and wheeled me to the lobby where I needed to go. He even made sure I was at the right spot. Then, he gave me his card and told me where to go to meet him when I was all done.

The staff at Abbott made sure I was registered. Abbott's check-in team had quite the process doing this. I wore a name tag like the one I had when I was in the hospital. After they gave me the name tag, they gave me all kinds of stickers that I was to give to the staff whenever I went somewhere. This was so the clinic could keep track of me, and all the tests I had gone through. After I received all this stuff, I found a spot to settle, and waited for Paula.

I contacted Paula. I wanted to tell her where I was so she could find me. She said she was running late, but would be there as soon as she could. I sat in the lobby, and waited for Paula and Jane, the research person, to find me.

I thought, whew, maybe I can rest. No such luck, Paula was right there. I was surprised she came so soon. If I would've had to find this spot, it would've taken hours. I was grateful for Paula coming early because it was strange sitting there by myself.

Paula said, "Jean, I need some more copies of your letter for my friends and Bible class."

Surprised at Paula's request, I said, "Really? Sure. I'll send you another copy on the computer e-mail."

Paula and I worked on this e-mail transfer, until Jane came. We greeted each other, and after introductions, we were off with the testing. So much for resting!

First, I signed consents and Jane read what I call this 25-page document of whatever's going to happen or could possibly happen during the infusion process of stem cells as they call it.

After I signed the consents, and listened to the document reading, my height, weight, and vitals were taken: only the basics, which were normal. Those studies tested me for everything. My height was 5'2¼," and my weight was 105 at this time. I can't remember my blood pressure. It still registered in the 90s/60s. Then, I answered questions as a health history, med list, etc.

During this testing, the effects of the trip started settling.

At one point, I was exhausted, and started having a major hot flash. Nurses are great. Jane sensed something was wrong right away.

Jane said, "Jean, do you want to lie down?"

Immediately, I shook my head yes, and chose to take advantage of her offer. I lay down for as long as I could!

I didn't pay too much attention to that reading document, I hate to admit. At one point, I actually heard Jane say I'd be awake for the infusion process, but my body would be numb, so I wouldn't feel a thing.

I said, "Wait a minute! I'm not so sure about this now."

Jane reiterated, "You won't feel a thing, but if you do, let them know right away, especially if the feeling lasts more than 3 minutes. If the sensation lasts for more than 3 minutes, they will slow down the infusion process."

She assured me that other patients who had that procedure did not feel a thing, and rested through it. After I heard Jane's explanation,

I thought, *Okay. They've done this a thousand times.* I didn't think too much more about it.

When Jane felt I was comfortable with the information I heard, she continued with the "Your rights" section of this study. One of those rights as my physician mentioned, was that I could back out of the study any time. After I heard that, I continued with the rest of the testing, since I was already there. I thought, *Well, I committed to it, and these guys obviously want to keep me alive.* Knowing I had the right to back out at any time gave me some control.

Jane said, "You can be disqualified by the test results too."

Instead of being all anxious about it, I decided I'd let the tests call the shots. If God wanted me to go through this infusion, He'd make it happen. Besides, I also wanted to help the team that had a part in saving my life. Jane continued reading the 25-page drill.

Jane said, "Dr. Henry will be coming at some point, but I don't know exactly the time. When he comes, we'll stop with wherever we are doing, so he can do his part. Then, when he finishes, we'll keep going from where we left off, and he can keep going with other patients."

Jane continued, "Wait until you meet Dr. Henry. He's amazing, and can remember people, events, and anything you want to know. He's great to work with."

We kept up with the reading of the rights until she heard his voice. Jane said, "Oh, I think he's coming, let me see."

Sure enough, incoming Dr. Henry.

Dr. Henry grabbed my chart and said, "New Ulm?" I smiled and said, "Yeah. That's me."

He came in the room, and I stood up to shake his hand, and said thank you. He actually was alright with receiving/giving hugs. In this day and age, you never know if you should hug anybody due to all the lawsuits with sex abuse scandals. A few tears rolled down my eyes. Dr. Henry sat down, and let me gain my composure.

Dr. Henry greeted my sister, Paula, who was also crying. Paula managed to ask Dr. Henry, "How do you like your new job?"

Dr. Henry smiled and went back to Jane to sign forms for her, so everything was all legal. When Dr. Henry finished signing papers, he said, "You gave us quite the scare."

He did a quick heart exam with his stethoscope and said, "Do you want to see the angiogram?"

I said, "Yeah— sure" (but at the same time I wondered what the heck he meant by an angiogram).

Dr. Henry asked one of the computer technicians if he'd set the pictures up on the screen and then said to me, "The room's around the corner. Are you able to walk that far?"

I said, "I think I can."

We went into a small room with lots of computers in it. Dr. Henry sat down and started the program. As Dr. Henry waited for the program to start up, he said, "Oh, a few people want to meet you and see this, is that okay?"

I said, "Sure. Anything if it helps."

Shortly after that, doctors, nurses, staff, and probably the whole research team came in. The room was full of doctors and staff.

Paula was behind me, and she had shed a few tears. We began to see how close to death I was, since all those doctors wanted to see how I was doing and what Dr. Henry had done.

Dr. Henry introduced me to a couple members of the team who were present the morning I arrived with my SCAD. I remembered one of them was Dave (different from my brother-in-law, Dave), who was in charge of the Cath lab.

Dave smiled and said, "Hi." I thought, I don't know what this Cath lab place is, but I must have been there.

I was overwhelmed, and I didn't say too much. I didn't want to sound ignorant or stupid in front of all those people.

Then Jane said, "Jean, do you want to sit down?" I said, "Yeah, thanks."

Jane found a chair for me, and I sat down right there next to Dr.

Henry. I was amazed as I sat next to Dr. Henry. At that point, he was like God in the fact that he saved my life!

While Dr. Henry continued setting the program up, he said, "What you did for New Ulm was great, and you're right, they did do a good job!"

I thought, *Okay. What great thing is he talking about that I had done for New Ulm?* Then I thought about what the Marketing and Communications Specialist person in New Ulm, Kitty, asked me about having permission to print my thankyou letter from the Journal in the Allina publication.

At first, I thought the Allina Hospital Kitty referred to only included New Ulm. After Dr. Henry's comment about the great thing I had done, I realized that Kitty printed my letter in a state-wide Allina publication, so Abbott received it. Otherwise, how else could Dr. Henry have known I wrote that thankyou? I didn't give him a copy.

I thought, *Oh boy! I wondered how many other Allina Hospitals there are in the state?*

Dr. Henry said, "You're right it does take a whole lot of people to care for one." Now I thought, *What did I get myself into?* When I realized that must've been exactly what happened (Kitty printed my letter in an Allina publication and Abbott received it), I tried to think of something clever to say.

I said, "Just so you know, Louise and I did spell Abbott with two ts."

Dr Henry smiled. I had no idea my little thankyou was going to go this far, and do all this good! It was only a little thankyou! Dr. Henry continued and said, "You had a spontaneous coronary artery dissection, SCAD. His definition of my condition verified what the cardiologist told me while I was in the hospital.

After I heard that diagnosis from him, I said point blank, "What did I do? I don't ever want this again?"

Dr. Henry said, "You can't and you won't. We can't predict this or prevent it."

During this conversation, Dr. Henry confirmed what the cardiologist in the hospital said about the rarity of my condition, and that Abbott only received three to five SCAD cases a year.

Dr. Henry said, "Patients with left main SCAD [which is what I had] is the one with the highest death rate, as they don't arrive at medical centers fast enough."

Paula said, "That's what the cardiologist said that Jean had when he came out to speak to us after her surgery."

After Dr. Henry heard us talk about what the cardiologist told our family after my surgery, he asked, "Who was the cardiologist?"

I said, "Dr. Knicklebine."

He shook his head yes, and said, "Well, he's right!"

I knew whatever I had was life threatening. I thought, *Huh?* I was shocked that God would choose me to have something as big as a Near-Death Experience but also live to tell about it. After all, it was just me, Jean Nielsen. I'm not a famous person nor had lots of wealth, let alone any clout at all. Why on earth would God choose someone like me to live, and tell about an experience like this? Who am I to think I had any way of convincing anyone of anything, especially something as big as this?

Even after I heard how rare my condition was, there was still no way I was about to tell Dr. Henry or Jane about any of this yet— my Near-Death Experience, that is. Besides, there were too many people around now. Plus, I was back up at Abbott. The last thing I wanted was them thinking I was a nut, and then commit me to the psych ward!

I was grateful to learn about the rarity of my condition. The rarity confirmed that my situation was life threatening, especially because cardiologists couldn't predict or prevent what I had. I prayed I hadn't done anything too stupid to my body, this gift, that God gave me.

Okay, the beers I drank and cigarettes I smoked weren't the smartest ideas ever that I had abused my body with, but gratefully, I was never addicted to them. Plus, at that point in my life, I drank and smoked because, it was a social thing, the "in thing" to do to be cool or popular.

Anyway, I was healthy for the age of 52 at the time of my heart attack. As it's written, I did not smoke, was not overweight, and had low cholesterol levels. After all, here's proof from the tests before my heart attack. I was a normal healthy 52-year old female.

I also joined Curves, a female fitness club, in 2003, and worked out 3x a week/12 x month total for half an hour each session. At first, I joined for profit. If I worked out 12x a month, my insurance would cover $20.00 of my cost.

The additional benefit of joining Curves was that a lady from HSI I worked with wanted to join. By going with her, I was paid for my time. I joined Curves as a win-win situation for me financially. I sealed my decision to join, because lo and behold, the manager was a Packer fan.

It was great to have the support at Curves and having a Packer fan as the manager made working out quite fun! Little did I know, by joining a fitness club, how much of a health impact working out would have on my life! I only joined as a benefit to my financial situation.

God does have a strange way of doing things! Just when I thought I was doing something for myself that was my decision, I realized, my decision came from God. It's always from God!

After I tried to grasp all this information from Dr. Henry, he explained the rest of the angiogram. Basically, I didn't understand it. It was like my brain was almost turned off. Dr. Henry continued and said, "First, I put a breathing tube in you as soon as you landed."

I thought, What! I was awake. I talked or sort of talked to the nurse in the helicopter. At least, I responded to his question, by shaking my head yes about my hearing aids.

After the helicopter nurse removed my hearing aids, I remembered thinking about the pretty amber glow from the lights I saw in the Cities. After the helicopter dropped three times, I thought *"Well, whatever's going to happen, is going to happen now, and I hope I did some good."*

That was my last thought when I was on earth, my last thought. While I watched this angiogram, I was amazed that my life came

down to mere seconds that depended on someone else to care for me and make life choices.

Then Dr. Henry said, "Once I got in with the angioplasty, I had two choices. I guessed, picked the right choice and kept going."

I could see the artery that was affected tearing on the screen, and he pointed different things out. I could also see how the stents opened after he inserted them in or around the artery or whatever he does to them.

At that point, I was also amazed to learn that the top cardiologist at Abbott had to guess as far as what to do with me after he got in with the angiogram. **GUESS!** The top cardiologist at Abbott had to **guess!** That can't be a coincidence!

Dr. Henry admitting that he had to guess as to what to do with me, made me think more about this book Marion gave me. I had read enough of the book by the time we arrived at Abbott to learn for a person to have a Near-Death Experience, two criteria must be confirmed: the condition must be rare, and life-threatening. Because of Dr. Henry's explanation on the rarity of my condition (only having 3-5 cases a year), and how life threatening (having to guess as to what to do with me, and that only 2-3 cases live), those facts justified my calling, my visit with God, a Near-Death Experience.

If a surgeon, especially the top cardiologist at Abbott, had to guess at anything as to what to do with me, that alone was enough to justify my condition being life-threatening and rare.

After Dr. Henry explained what he did to me, he asked, "Do you have any more questions?"

I shook my head no. Then Dr. Henry said, "Are you up for a picture?"

I gave him a funny look and he added, "They like to take pictures for these studies, especially with my case being rare, life threatening, and the fact that I was the last recipient in this phase."

I was honored to have a picture taken with Dr. Henry. We went down to the Abbott NW sign at the front. Jane pushed me in a wheel chair as it was quite far. About a half-dozen people were taking pictures, and if I do say so myself it turned out pretty good! This is a phenomenon as I usually take bad pictures!

On our way to take pictures, I discovered more surprises. As we left the computer room, the staff were lined up all the way down the hallway. The staff clapped and cheered for me! Computer screens lined the hallways, so no matter where staff were, they could see the program Dr. Henry was using.

I knew what Jane meant in her thankyou letter that I'd be enthusiastically thanked. Primarily, the thank you was due more to the fact that I was willing to participate in this study than my case being that big a deal. Pretty sneaky.

I felt I had done something good since all those people wanted to meet me. I cried a few more tears from this act of appreciation. I didn't think my case was that important, but it must have been for all those people to take the time out of their schedules to meet me.

After taking pictures, Dr. Henry finished my exam and said, "You're doing great. Maybe you're already pumping at 40%. I don't know, but we'll see." I wasn't sure what he meant by that 40% comment, and we never discussed it. Dr. Henry said, "Goodbye and we'll see you soon." And, yes, he gave me another hug.

Once he left, Jane completed the 25-page research document. She said, "I know, it's boring, but I have to read it verbatim."

Before Jane continued, Paula said, "So, it really was a guessing game?"

Jane shook her head yes. I said, "What made him keep going on me?"

Jane said, "He guessed and guessed right. Had he gone in the other way, he would've had to have given up. They probably did a cheer in the operating room when they got done."

After Jane's explanation, Paula and I thought, Wow! Death was that close. Paula started crying, again. In my mind, Dr. Henry's explanations of the rarity and how he acted so quickly to save me definitely confirmed how close to death I had been and that my visit with God was **real**.

I was relieved at Dr. Henry's and Jane's explanations, because I knew that I was with God! I don't care what anybody else wants to call my experience, but having Dr. Henry's and Jane's explanations was enough medical proof to justify my calling, my visit with God, a N*ear-Death Experience.* I was relieved, too, because I could put a name to *My Visit with God.*

Jane continued to explain the Stem Cell procedure in layman's terms. While she was reading that 25-page document, she told me I could have a snack, since I had a couple hours before the MRI. After the document reading, Jane pushed me to the lobby where Paula and I waited for the next tests. The clock showed us that it was around noon, and I only had an ECHO, MRI, and Holter monitor fitting left. The ECHO went fine. That measured how well my heart was pumping.

Before going to the MRI, Paula was interrupted with work and said, "Jean, are you okay now? I should take care of this."

Jane said, "I'll take you where you need to go."

I said, "Yeah, go ahead. I'm okay."

The last MRI wasn't bad, so I felt comfortable going in there. Thankfully, my hot flashes had subsided, so I wouldn't feel like I was burning up or that I was in a coffin. I was eager, and wanted to continue reading the book that Marion had given me, especially after hearing Dr. Henry's and Jane's explanations of the rarity of my condition. I wanted to find out more about those other Near-Death Experiences.

I had started reading that book, but the nurses in the MRI room had finished early with the other patients. I was next, so reading any part of that book wasn't going to happen. The MRI measured my infarct or size of the incision made where Dr. Henry inserted the stents, if I'm correct.

I was stabbed with IV needles and whatever, and the nurses injected dye into the needle tubing halfway through the process. I was used to MRIs by now, so this one seemed to go quickly.

Interestingly, the technician for the MRI was the same one I had with my first awful one. We laughed about that experience this time, but she still felt bad about it. I figured that if she learned from it, that was good enough for me. At least, I wasn't in danger.

The technician showed me where she would be and explained that there were always two people in the room, which definitely made me feel safer. We finished that process and had one last stop.

I needed a fitting for a Holter monitor. I was to wear that around my neck for 24 hours then drop it in the mail, so the research team could take whatever information they needed. That needed to be done before the infusion of stem cells the following week.

After the monitor fitting, which thankfully was rather painless, Jane came for me. I called my driver and told him everything was done. He said to meet him at the front lobby.

Jane wheeled me down to McDonald's, and while doing so, made a comment on the book I had. I told her I had received it from one of the ladies on our church's prayer chain. Marion, who loaned me the book, thought perhaps the experience I had at Abbott was one of those that the author Eban Alexander had.

When Jane and I arrived to meet the driver, the other passenger was already there. She had her book with her. Jane happened to ask her what the name of her book was. She started telling us what was in it, and how good it was. It sounded a lot like my book.

After she told us about her book, I pulled mine out. I said, "Is this it?"

She pulled out hers and said, "Yeah! It is!"

Jane said, "You two have the same book? Do you know each other?" We shook our heads no.

Then, I realized two of us having the same book was another sign from God that it was okay for me to keep sending out *My Visit with God* letter. The very concern I had had on the way up to the Cities about whether I should have shared my story was answered through others.

How ironic that two complete strangers both had the same book. Of course, we know that nothing is ironic. Yep, that's how God used others to encourage me that it was okay to keep sharing my story.

We left the Cities around 4:30 p.m. By the time we arrived in New Ulm, it was around 6-6:30 p.m. I called Louise, and she came and picked me up. I ate supper and went to bed early that night. As I was exhausted from the day's events and didn't sleep well the night before. It was good to sleep in the next day, too.

On Thursday, September 26th, 2013, a call came in from Abbott. The number was very recognizable by now. I was nervous about all this stem cell information. But, I knew if God wanted me to have the Stem Cell infusion done, it would be done. The call was from Jane.

Jane said, "Jean, I have some disappointing news. The test results came back and we have to disqualify you from the study."

I almost fainted. I said, "What! Really! How?"

Jane explained, "Your heart has to be pumping at less than 40%, which is what the ECHO showed. You heart was pumping at 40.6%." After I heard that test result, I thought, O*h, that must've been what Dr. Henry meant about my heart already pumping at 40%.*

Jane continued with the results and said, "Not only that, but your scar tissue had to be over 15%, as that's indicative of future heart issues. Your MRI showed your scar tissue at 12.6%, which is just under what you need to qualify."

I said, "I can't believe it!"

Jane said, "We were so surprised, too! Patients who've had one or two stents have qualified for stem cells. I canceled your room and cath lab appointments, but we are so glad for you! You can drop the Holter monitor in a mail box, and we'll get it." I never did figure out what that was for!

After I heard those test results, I remembered what I thought earlier about whether God wanted me to do the research. I thought for sure I'd qualify for the study. Seriously, a condition as rare as mine, surviving with seven stents down the main artery of my heart (a procedure that had never been done), and I don't qualify for stem cell research. You can't have a health situation any rarer than that!

Plus, I was even the last recipient in the safety phase of this study before they could move on to the next phase: the last recipient! Were all of those circumstances coincidences? C'mon! I don't think so!

Once again, God told me I didn't need to do this infusion, and I went through this experience for other reasons. I decided the reasons must be the ones I came up with in the hospital, to write thethankyou in the Letter to the Editor, and share *My Visit with God* with others to convince them that God and Heaven exist. They exist! Whew, I had already done that, so my jobs must be done.

I felt bad that the research team couldn't use me after they spent all that time and money on me, but didn't say this. Jane asked, "Can I keep your case in a data base? Maybe something else will come up in the future."

I said, "Sure! Go ahead."

After learning about the stem cell research and going through the screening, I realized that if I needed to have an infusion later, it didn't seem quite as scary, even if I had to stay awake for the infusion process. At least, I would be somewhat healthier anyway.

During that conversation with Jane, I asked, "What do I do about the October 2, appointment?"

Jane said, "I'll check, but I figure you should go up and meet with Dr. Traverse, as you do need to make routine appointments with a cardiologist."

I said, "Okay."

We said our well wishes and goodbyes. The following day, Jane called and said, "Yes, you should definitely keep the appointment on October 2 with Dr. Traverse."

I said, "I know Dr. Henry's gone, but I'd still like to write a thank you to you and him if I can connect with you then."

Jane said, "Sure, I know when your appointment is, so I will come and find you."

I thought, Whew, since I know who Dr. Henry, and Jane are, they should have a thank you and a letter about my Near-Death Experience. Even if they don't believe in God, they might like to know what else happened with my Near-Death Experience, since they are professionals, in case someone else might have had an experience like mine. Plus, they'll understand why I seemed so nervous about everything!

We said our goodbyes, and I made more transportation arrangements to the Cities for the following week.

I was definitely glad I had written my letter to the editor, *My Visit with God,* and shared them. My jobs were done, and I needed to have a somewhat normal life routine back.

The question still nagged me on what my experience was called, and the area I was in while I with God. I still wanted a term for what my experience was called: a concrete term, especially from somebody more qualified than I was to "coin" those experiences. That experience was too big for anyone to call it anything, especially a Near-Death Experience, a subject that was very controversial, and a topic of which I knew nothing. I wanted a professional to call it something. However, to what professional do I go?

I started to recap all the information I had. I wanted to make sure all of the spiritual and medical steps were covered, so I could call my experience a Near-Death Experience. I needed to do that for my own sake.

People continued to call to see how I was and many sent gifts and cards. Gifts of food, flowers, and prayers came from people we met in

TEC, a retreat program for those wanting to grow closer to Christ-Together Encounter Christ. parishioners, and cousins.

See Stories at the Back

After disqualifying for Stem Cell Research, I was still in definite AWE of the whole experience. I was not in any way, shape, or form qualified to term my visit with God as a Near-Death Experience from a personal stand-point, but I felt like it definitely was one: at least, I could call it one. Others told me that's what it was, and I started calling it one.

I continued to doubt my visit with God as a Near-Death Experience because I had no professional or spiritual term; yet that was my fault as I was too insecure to ask either ministers or doctors in those professions about my experience. In my own mind, because I had not heard about such experiences, I was too engulfed with fear of Hell or other frightening consequences or in being ridiculed or diagnosed as insane by asking about an experience that was taking over all my waking moments.

After all, I had discovered that Heaven was real, but on the flip side, I also discovered that Hell was real, and NOBODY should ever want to go there or send somebody else there. I eventually received the spiritual direction I had feared to seek, and that removed away all of my fear.

CHAPTER 17:

MIRACLES

AUNT TUB, A sister of the Holy Names of Jesus and Mary (SNJM), was out in California so, wouldn't be able to commit me to a psych ward in Minnesota if she thought I was a nut! I still didn't want to talk to our priest without a term for what I had, as I was afraid he might think I was a nut. Okay. That's it! I called my Aunt Tub to find out what I had.

While I talked to Aunt Tub, I asked about what terms I should use as to what to call my experience, and how the church declared experiences as miracles!

Aunt Tub said, "You could call it whatever you want because it's your experience. A miracle is something that happens as a result of an experience that wasn't supposed to happen to allow the person to live/heal or whatever. It doesn't necessarily have to be life-threatening.

For instance, I had my eye replaced years back, as I was going blind. I wasn't supposed to see, and from the eye replacement, I had recovered fully. I call that surgery a miracle. You have to prepare yourself somewhat. I was learning the guitar, and crafts to give me something to do in case I was permanently blind. In your case, you couldn't have done this [prepared yourself] as you had no idea your issue was going to come up, and you were out for two days. Nobody knew what was going to happen to you for two days! You are a Miracle!

I believed Aunt Tub was biased, though, she spoke with deep conviction and love. Still, it was nice to hear I could do something GREAT, even if I didn't plan or set out to do it. In a way, it was kind of scary to be called great or a miracle, a tough ideal to live up to. Then, she touched on another topic of which I was unfamiliar.

Aunt Tub said, "You are a *witness to prayer,* because prayer brought you back."

Next, Aunt Tub explained sort of where I was, but she didn't call this room anything or any place.

Aunt Tub said, "You weren't in Heaven, though, because you can't go to Heaven and come back."

Now, I'm confused again. Just when I was convinced I can justify that I had a Near-Death Experience, Aunt Tub rejected it. How could I have all those medical and spiritual coincidences "happen", but not call my visit with God a Near-Death Experience?

After Aunt Tub explained that I can't go to Heaven and come back, I realized she was right. The room I was in couldn't have been Heaven, because I looked up to God when I asked Him, "To borrow a little bit more time, because Lola and Emily need their Grandma Jean?" I wasn't on an even plane as He, so to speak; not that I should've been, but I was too far down to be in Heaven, because I was looking up to God. I was definitely looking up.

Not that I've ever been in that room before, but my own understanding was if I were in Heaven, I'd be closer to the clouds. I was not. I was stuck. Stuck in an area with nowhere to go.

For the sake of argument, I assumed my aunt was right. I could understand the point that I couldn't go to Heaven and come back. I believed Heaven would be a place so beautiful and perfect, I wouldn't want to even think about asking to come back, even if it meant not having any more time with our grandchildren. I couldn't imagine, being in Heaven and asking to come back.

Okay, Aunt Tub was right. I wasn't in Heaven, but then where? After Aunt Tub neglected to justify my visit with God as a Near-Death Experience or that I was in Heaven, I wondered again what that experience was called, and where I was. How would I ever convince people God and Heaven exist, if I don't even know how to explain it myself!

CRAP! I thought I'd have all the answers talking to Aunt Tub, because she was going to call my experience a Near-Death Experience and tell me I was in Heaven, and for sure she was going to back me up. She's my aunt! She'd give me the church's perspective on miracles, a term to the name of my experience, and the area in which I was. Those reasons were going to justify my experience as a Near-Death Experience. NO SUCH LUCK THERE! What's the matter with clergy anyway? No wonder I felt intimidated talking to clergy!

Frankly, I should've left naming my experience alone. I should never have asked Aunt Tub what this experience was called. She may have even made it worse telling me I could name my experience whatever I wanted, because she was clergy. Now, I would have to start all over again to figure out what to call it. Boy, wait till I see Aunt Tub again! I'm going to have a bone to pick with her.

I was back at square one trying to name the area I was in, when I was having my experience with God. However, now that my story's out and people know about it, I'm frustrated that I still can't put a name to it. Not naming my experience or wherever that place was when I was in with God, frustrated me to no end.

My aunt disturbed me by not naming my experience. But, on the upswing, she did define the church's position on what a miracle was, and called *me* a Miracle! I was definitely somewhere in between Earth and Heaven. But calling *me* a Miracle! *Me?* Sure!

Eban Alexander also wrote that everyone's experience is different. Maybe he called his experience a Near-Death Experience, because like Aunt Tub said, "You can call it (the experience) anything you like. It's your experience." Yes. Maybe that's what he called the room he was in according to him, Heaven, his Heaven. Not the "real" Heaven, but his Heaven? I don't know.

Other reasons counteracted with my calling, my visit, a Near-Death Experience. Primarily, authors of Near-Death Experiences were non-believers in God. In comparing mine to Eban Alexander's book, he said he didn't truly believe in God. He never refuted any patient's beliefs of God, but he himself wasn't a true believer. Well, I already believed in God and Heaven! Why on earth would I need an experience, if I already believed in God? There was no reason to justify my having a Near-Death Experience. I already believed, and was serving God the best I knew how.

Another obvious reason counteracted with my having a Near-Death Experience. Authors of Near-Death Experiences had clout, and a position of power within their employment. Obviously, someone with clout and power could easily convince others God and Heaven exist.

Who am I to think I could convince anyone of those facts: that God and Heaven exist, a topic of such a controversial nature. Again, I had no clout nor position of power in my employment. I was only a Direct Support Professional (DSP) at a group home and a Resident Care Provider (RCP) at an assisted living facility. Neither position had any clout.

During my conversation with Aunt Tub, she told me, "Everyone I showed your letter to who knew our family, believed it. Nobody doubted it."

I thought, Yeah, at least, she BELIEVED ME! I'm safe. My aunt who is a nun believes me!

I can't remember how Aunt Tub and I ended our conversation. I was not in a listening mode, probably because I learned about being a witness to prayer, and was still trying to figure out what my experience was called, where I was, and the concept that I was a miracle! Honestly, I don't know how, but at some point, Aunt Tub and I said our goodbyes.

I decided, at the very least, to call the place where I encountered God, a room. That was all I had for naming it, and that was better than nothing! I was relieved and grateful that Aunt Tub believed me! She believed I was somewhere, and that I was with GOD! I decided instead of worrying about what to call my experience or where I was, it was time to move on with my life.

I focused on how I was going to fulfill my response to God. I remembered my response seemed pretty vague. Fulfilling my response could only be accomplished by having more of a life routine. Now that my physical self was well, I needed to discern what I may have intended in my response that I could still be a better person when God asked, "What are you going to do for me?"

CHAPTER 18:

THE ANSWER

Well, God asked, **"What are you going to do for me?"** I responded, "I could still be a better person."

At first, my response was only a statement. I wasn't sure if there was a specific answer to my response. The phrase that I could still be a better person was said for the same reason, to save my skin. I remembered, I wasn't going to state what more I was going to do for God in case I couldn't follow through with it. My response was a way to keep my earthly body.

Then that song I heard when I was in that area kept playing in my mind. The lyrics reminded of how the entire Earth in all its splendor praises and worships God: the people, the mountains, and the seas. God promised Heaven and untold glories to those who love Him. I tried desperately to figure out what God was telling me with those lyrics.

Our daughter, Louise, had a lot of Christian music. One day, she was visiting us with our granddaughter. I said, "Louise do you know the name of this song?" I tried to sing the lyrics to her that I had heard.

Louise knew right away and shook her head yes. "It's *Shout to the Lord*."

I said, "Do you have a copy? It's been going on in my head, and I can't remember the lyrics?"

Louise said, "Sure."

The next time she came over, she brought it.

I said, "Yes! That's it. Can I keep it for a while?" Louise said, "Sure."

Louise didn't ask any more questions about the music. That was good, because I didn't know what I was going to be doing with it anyway. At that point, I was excited to have the rest of the lyrics.

My first thought about hearing those words were maybe I should to start playing the piano again, and that's why God gave me another chance to keep my earthly body. I played some warm-up scales and some old classical pieces. I felt good to play the piano again, but I was definitely rusty.

I felt the urge to keep up with the piano anyway. After all, I had around 8 years of lessons and was pretty good after playing in music contests. I kept up with learning that song. Since I wasn't playing the song any better on the piano, I decided to learn the rest of the lyrics. As I learned the lyrics, I focused on their meaning. I thought maybe there's something in the words I was supposed to hear?

The first few times I played that song, I cried, especially during the part of the refrain when it says how the whole Earth worships God.

One night in early September, I was incredibly frustrated not knowing how I could still be a better person. Before I went to bed, I prayed to God for the answer. When I woke the next morning, the sun's rays were beaming all over my body, as they came pouring through the window.

I had a strange, peaceful feeling around me, but I felt freaky, at the same time, because I couldn't move. I thought I was paralyzed. It was early, around 7:00 a.m. I had those lyrics I heard when I was with God going through my mind quite loudly.

As I lay in bed, I heard more of the lyrics. I asked myself why I was hearing those words. That could have been because I had been playing the song on the piano, I don't know, but more words came.

As more words came, so, did the answer to my response to God's question! In the past, I had briefly lost focus on God. I had that experience twenty years ago. I decided then, that I wasn't going to doubt God's intentions and plans for me again. I had forgotten that I was on Earth to know, love, and serve God: not myself.

As I discovered the answer to my response to God's question, I thought, *that's it, that's how I could still be a better person.* The nagging feeling I had while I tried to find the answer was gone, because I had found the answer in those lyrics. I had forgotten why I was here again. Now, I remembered. God told me exactly how I was going to be a better person by using that song. I would praise Him and worship Him on His terms: not mine!

Now that I had the answer to my response to God's question, it seemed ridiculous that I needed a Near-Death Experience to remember what I was supposed to be doing all this time. I should've been doing that anyway. Actually, I thought I was. Evidently, I was missing something in my life, though.

Since I had the answer, I needed to put it into practice. Putting the answer into practice was easier said than done. I tried to put the ANSWER into practice right away.

Living as God instructed involved more work than I realized. I needed to take a step-by-step look at the answer to my response , not in all the areas I chose, but in all the areas of my life.

Chapter 19:

More Important Firsts

Back to Mass

Around the end of September, 2013 after stem cell research and my first outing, I felt up to trying to attend Mass. Knowing it was going to take a while, we headed out around 4:30 p.m. for 5:30 p.m. Mass. Thankfully, our church has a drive-up entrance for the elderly or physically impaired. I never thought I'd be the one using that feature!

Rod walked with me into the church and settled me in the old cry room. Then, he went to park the car. While I waited for him, our priest happened to see me. He said, "Welcome back. I hear you are a miracle!"

I smiled and said, "Thank you," or something to that effect. I didn't have the heart to tell him I yelled for him when I was out as I thought he might think I'm a nut yet. To date, I still haven't had enough nerve to tell him that story. Maybe one day I will. Maybe.

When Rod came back, finding a pew was the next order of business. Our church serves more than 1,300 families. It's oval in nature and people usually sit in their same pews. Sitting in the same pews is typical in Catholic churches. Nobody seems to know the reason for this. One priest up north said at a Mass though, "It's because people like the other people who generally sit in the same pews." I'll use that as reasoning. We usually sat in the middle on the right, so when I distributed Communion, I had a quick route to the altar.

Instead of sitting in our usual section at Mass, we sat toward the back where the elderly and disabled sat, to have an easy access out if needed. Sitting in that section was an eye-opener for me. It was a nice change in a way. The change gave me a different perspective of what goes on at the altar, and how clear I could hear.

I could tell parishioners wondered what I was doing in that section by the quizzical looks on their faces. They knew where I sat, and had seen me many times serving/setting up for Mass.

As I was walking in to sit down, one of the other sacristans was coming with the tray. She stopped and said, "Jean, how are you? We couldn't believe what we heard about you. We got your letter, and it was so moving. We were praying for you."

She and her husband sent a get-well card, so I sent a thank you with a letter to them. Even more prayers were being said for me. Before Mass, another couple, good friends of ours, sat in the back

with us. They sent me a card, so they had received a thank you with *My Visit with God* letter. I got a big hug from both of them. They asked, "How are you doing? We couldn't imagine it was you when we heard you had a heart attack." I was so glad to see them, and that seemed reciprocal.

When Mass ended, another couple came up, and talked to me as Rod was getting the car. They are Packer fans and go to the bowling alley on Sundays to watch the Packer games (as we do). They had seen the thank you that I had published in the paper. They were shocked upon hearing about my heart attack, and had wondered why I hadn't been at the bowling alley lately. Packer fans become like family to people in New Ulm, Minnesota!

We had a guest speaker at Mass who was from Owatanna, Minnesota. Rod said, "Jean, you have to meet this guy."

I thought, *Why? I'm pooped.* As it turned out, the person I was supposed to meet was the guest speaker.

He said, "Jean, we've been praying for you for a month already!" I said, "What! You have? How did you know about me?"

He said, "Your daughter called us and told us what happened. We started praying for you right away. The speaker added, "Your daughter's father-in-law told us about how your condition being so rare, and the procedure you survived with seven stents had never been done. He called you a miracle!"

I immediately thought, Wow, more prayers from another city we had no association with, and from people I didn't even know. I thought I had all the prayers accounted for. Nope, not yet, and probably not ever.

I had a few tears come, but I held them back. I thought the whole time during that conversation how PEOPLE ARE GREAT! Still, I didn't know what I had done to deserve all those prayers!

The next weekend at Mass, we parked on the street, and another couple who had caught my thank you in the paper stopped us. They were surprised and glad to see me come back. Since they sat in the same area where we usually did, we greeted each other before every Mass.

Then a physician assistant from the New Ulm Medical Center stopped me after Mass and said she had read my letter in the Allina publication.

She said, "It was so nice to see your article, and I really appreciated it."

Rod and I asked, "Do you think New Ulm will ever offer stenting?" She said, "No. It's really not the design of the hospital. Stenting is very expensive and you have to have a cardiologist on-call 24 hours."

Our church was having its Fall Festival that week. I couldn't help at the take-out meals, but Rod worked. One parishioner, who worked at the clinic, visited with Rod while she helped at the take-out meals.

She noticed I was missing, and asked Rod how I was doing. She sent a card, and after that, and I sent her a thank you and letter too.

The whole month of October went by before I walked into the church from the street, and up to Communion by myself. I walked that far, because I participated in cardio rehab, although I didn't want to admit that cardio rehab worked.

Since our church is quite large, at the end of Communion, our priest brings the Sacrament to those who can't walk to the front. I realized one day I would be sitting in those back pews one day, but not at such a young age. The parishioners who sit there came up after Mass and greeted me.

They said, "We were so surprised when we heard about you. We [all] prayed for you."

Some parishioners read my article in the Journal or received and made a copy of *My Visit with God*. Frankly, it had been copied by now hundreds of times.

I was pleasantly surprised at the positive response *My Visit with God* had, because I never knew how people felt about those experiences. Maybe the difference in my experience being so widely accepted was partly that I only wanted people to understand how God heard their prayers, their prayers worked, and made a difference.

I hadn't actually labeled the experience anything. Come to think of it, maybe that's why I struggled with calling my experience something for such a long time. Instead of worrying about what to name it, I was supposed to focus on the meaning of the experience and sharing it. So many times we all feel like we need to define and name things—maybe we only need to experience things, and not worry about so much about defining them!

Other good friends of ours came up after Mass, and asked how I was doing. We had met through a charismatic retreat one night quite a few years back. The woman and I had started talking, and we hit it right off. She was a teacher, too, which helped. I was so grateful to hear that she called it a Near-Death Experience mainly, because now I could call it something.

They were well-known in New Ulm so to hear her call it a Near-Death Experience made me feel relieved, and grateful. They sent some flowers, and a card when they heard I was home. They were beautiful.

The most common words people used to describe my visit with God were "moving/inspirational." Many people also said that my account gave them goosebumps or cried when they read it. But the tears were good, because they felt comforted, especially if they had lost someone.

More often than not, everyone who received a copy sent one to at least one person. I was so grateful to hear that response mostly, because more people received a copy; many of whom I didn't know, and it reassured me that my Near-Death-Experience was real. YEAH! Whew! It pays to know people, I tell ya!

One parishioner told me that the reason she believed my Near-Death Experience (NDE) was real was, because she knew me. She had read books or seen movies about Near-Death Experiences, but, because she had not known those people, she wasn't convinced that their experiences were real. However, knowing me, as she did, gave her new insights and consequently to believe.

At that time, books about Near-Death Experiences were being published, and the movie, "Heaven is for Real" was released. Because of those books and movies, believing in my experience made it easier for people to accept and trust that my Near-Death Experience was real!

Please! If anyone ever tells you about his/her Near-Death Experience, encourage that person to share it. Don't doubt it. Trust me! That person already thinks he/she is nuts! I know! Sharing those experiences with others is one way to communicate to people that GOD EXISTS AND HEAVEN EXISTS!

Remember, Aunt Tub said that everyone she showed my letter to and "who knew our family believed!" They believed, and then they showed it to others. When people know others who have gone through an experience, it becomes personal for them. REAL! The more people hear about Near-Death Experiences from those they know, who have gone through one, the more they will believe GOD EXISTS AND HEAVEN EXISTS!

Hearing about Near-Death Experiences from someone they know is like first-hand knowledge for them. Who better really to hear about a topic like that or any topic for that matter, with such a controversial viewpoint, then from someone you know: someone you know and trust.

Remember, more copies of my Visit with God were being shared, because friends asked if they could share the letter with their families. Their comments on wanting to share my letter led me to adding my permission to the other thankyous I wrote, for others to share my letter as well. I thought, too, *PEOPLE ARE GREAT!* Those comments also made me feel incredibly relieved, and glad I sent it out.

Ironically, sharing my experience with others was more inspirational for me than for those with whom I shared it. I was amazed to hear how my Near-Death Experience affected adults, especially,because I never thought I had any impact on them: ADULTS! Me, just an average Catholic-born, Wisconsin-native, German, Irish, Swiss, Luxembourger, GreenBay Packer fan! I have neither clout nor status and yet, adults believed in me more than I believed in myself.

Yes, sharing *My Visit with God* Letter *was inspirational, and meant more to me than anyone could ever imagine.* Going back to Mass after my rehab led to changes in different aspects of my spiritual life.

In my spiritual life, I continued to pray the Rosary but the responsibilities shifted. Instead of being the parishioner who was a follower, I became the leader. When I started going back to church after cardio rehab, I began leading the Rosary at the Cathedral on Monday afternoons.

The next week, the lady who had led the Rosary couldn't make it. Another said, "Here! I want you to have this Rosary. You should lead. But the Rosary's not blessed."

I said, "Thank you. Are you sure you want me to lead?" She said, "Oh yes!"

I said, "The Rosary beads you gave me are more special and blessed than you know!"

Her asking me to lead the Rosary was a strong sign that we needed to keep it going, and I needed to lead the prayer when I could. So, I led, and have been helping to lead when possible. I use the Rosary she gave me every time I lead it at the Cathedral. I specifically used that Rosary at that time, and undoubtedly, it was the best spiritual gift I was given! I'm doing pretty good at leading.

The next Saturday, a woman from St. Mary's called to see if I'd lead the Rosary before the Mass at St. Mary's. So, I lead the Rosary there, and will probably be called again when they need help. How interesting that both churches needed somebody the same week to lead the Rosary!

I also signed up to take the Eucharist to the home bound!

I didn't go back to my sacristan duties for a while, because the church had started a remodeling project. Mass was being held in the basement for the winter, and I didn't want to tackle all those stairs. I wasn't a big fan of elevators! Consequently, I held off with my sacristan duties, but I was okay with this. However, I felt that my spiritual life was somewhat reorganized.

One piece of my life was reorganized: my spiritual life. My jobs were done, my letter was written, my thank you was out, and my spiritual life was completed, since I was going back to church.

I thought I had completed what I told God I was going to do to be a better person, after writing the letter to the editor, and sharing my Visit With God letter to others, but I felt like I continued the need to do more: something was missing.

The feeling was the same as in the book, The Grinch Who Stole Christmas, by Dr. Seuss when the Grinch discovered that as the true meaning of Christmas meant *just a little bit more* for the Whos' rather than only needing the material items to celebrate it; I felt perhaps my experience had a deeper meaning as well rather than only sharing my story the ways that I had. I brushed off the feeling for a while, and then thought, *Yep! PEOPLE ARE GREAT! THEY ARE TRULY GREAT!*

Now, I needed to organize the other areas of my life. The next step in putting my life together was mobility. I needed to be more independent. Driving was the next logical step. I decided to ask Clarice about that driving business next time I went to rehab.

CHAPTER 20:

BACK TO CARDIO REHAB 2

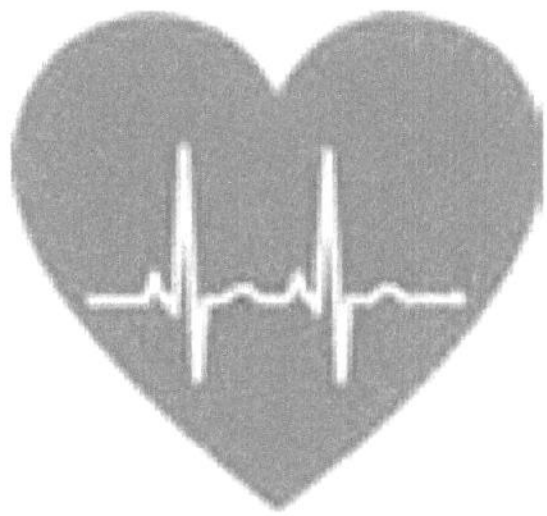

On Friday, September 27, 2013, I checked with Clarice about driving, because I was tired and wasn't sure about taking control of the wheel. I was stronger, and I had started walking through the parking lot to rehab while pushing our granddaughter in the stroller.

Because I had walked into the hospital, I thought I was ready to drive. To be safe, I wanted to double check with Clarice.

Clarice said, "As long as you're not on narcotics, it's okay to drive." When I started driving, Rod reassured me that he thought I was doing fine. I'm not sure if he was saying that to convince himself or

me, but it helped.

Rose was my next victim. Rose came home one weekend to see Louise's kids. Since it was close to lunch, I said, "Let's go to Subway for lunch. I'll drive!"

Rose was up for the challenge, realizing, of course, that I had already had one lesson with her dad. I drove safely out, and she even said the same thing as her dad that I was doing fine really.

After driving with Rod and Rose, I thought I'd try driving alone. I felt comfortable driving to rehab. After all, the New Ulm Medical

Center was only a couple blocks from home. I figured it was safe to drive that far anyway!

Now that I was driving in town with the help of Rose and Rod, I needed to continue getting well and to think about going back to work. That would be a good question for my new cardiologist.

CHAPTER 21:

BACK TO ABBOTT STORY

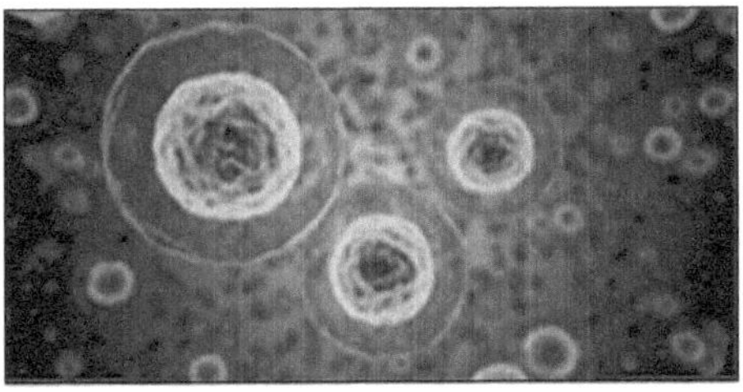

Wednesday, October 2, 2013

EVEN THOUGH I had had a couple of driving trips, I wasn't ready for a trip to the Cities. Our daughter Rose was home, so she drove me to my first cardiology appointment. I wasn't quite sure what to expect meeting my new cardiologist. Dr. Henry's nurse said Dr. Traverse was a gentle soul. She described him perfectly: more quiet and calm than Dr. Henry. They both had great rapport with people, and I felt at ease, no matter what kind of questions I asked. They both remembered health events. I was amazed because patients are usually identified with numbers, and that's it. No wonder they made a great team. They actually complemented one another.

Dr. Traverse came in and said, "You had quite the morning, when you came to see us the first time."

Dr. Traverse went over the results of the All Star study, and repeated how I was disqualified for the research. The conversation confirmed what Jane had said.

I asked him about going back to work.

Dr. Traverse said, "Go for it. Ask if you can go part time and see what happens."

He gave me a work slip with restrictions. I knew shopping, vacuuming, and shoveling would be impossible. I also wasn't sure about stairs. He wrote the back-to-work slip with those specifics, and I felt much better about going back to work.

After Dr. Traverse wrote the work restrictions, he updated my meds.

Dr. Traverse said, "I want your blood pressure to be 90/60s and even 85/60s if possible."

I was surprised at how low Dr. Traverse wanted my blood pressure numbers, because I already had low blood pressure. But, I wasn't about to argue with him. I knew better than to argue with anyone after trying with Clarice and Deb at cardio rehab!

Next, I asked about additional visits.

Dr. Traverse asked, "Do you have a cardiologist?" I said, "Well, not now. Do you go to New Ulm?"

Dr. Traverse said, "Yes, I go to New Ulm, and you could see me there. After a heart attack, we cardiologists want you to see us or your physician every 3 months for the next 2-5 years."

Having him come to New Ulm would be much better than driving to the Cities. I registered with him as my new cardiologist, and made some future appointments. Before I left, I thanked him.

Jane, the research study nurse, who had given me the news about disqualifying for the stem cell research, came and found me down in Dr. Traverse's office.

I said, "Thank you for finding me. Here are your thankyous I promised you. Hopefully, you'll like them." I gave her two thankyous.

Jane said, "I'm sure we will. I'll see that Dr. Henry gets his too." We gave hugs, and she greeted my daughter, Rose.

After I gave Jane the thankyous, we said goodbyes. Jane mentioned something again about putting me in a data base. I said, "Sure. You can use my information as long as you need to."

Rose and I stopped to eat then, drove to Paula's house to stay there for the night. We were too tired to drive back to New Ulm. Rose, and

I decided to take advantage of the day off and sleep in at Paula's. She and I arrived in New Ulm early the next afternoon, where I worked on more firsts.

Chapter 22:

More Firsts

Back to Work

Thursday, October 3, 2013— After that appointment, and the reality that bills started to accumulate, the next area of my life that needed to be arranged was easy to figure out: my work area. The first task was to contact the assisted living facility. This job was easier for me to start with as a work routine than HSI. I contacted the director when she returned from vacation, and met with her the next day.

At my October visits both my physician, Dr. Frannie Knowles and cardiologist, Dr. Traverse thought it'd be okay to go to the assisted living facility, but not HSI yet. I went to the assisted living facility, and visited with the director and staff who appeared glad to see me.

The director thought it would be fine to train with the gal I trained with initially. I gave her my work slip, and we visited. The director said, "I'm glad everything turned out okay. You could start next Sunday. If you needed more time, let me know."

I was surprised that my training went so well. Going back to the same shift, and the same place where I had experienced my SCAD felt eerie… and I feared I may have some Post-Traumatic Stress Disorder, PTSD, issues, but I felt rather peaceful.

The Care Provider (CP) Miranda and I visited, as it is quiet on the floor at night— most of the time. She was glad to see me and filled me in on the staff's reactions.

Miranda said, "The gal you relieved when you had your SCAD couldn't believe it. Everyone asked me if you looked any different, when you came to work that night. She said, "I looked fine! I hadn't noticed anything!"

We laughed. They didn't know I had a Near-Death Experience. I did not share this with anyone there, since I wasn't sure how they would respond with the residents, and because I was so new.

Miranda and I thought about other theories of why my heart attack might have happened at work. Miranda said, "What would've happened if you would've been at home?"

I said, "If my SCAD would have happened at the group home or at home, I wouldn't have survived! I wouldn't have called 911 at the group home, and Rod and I wouldn't have called them at home."

Miranda said, "Wow! That's weird. I suppose you would've been sleeping at both places too."

I agreed. Then I thought, No wonder God had me have my SCAD here. He knew I wouldn't have reacted the same way at any other place.

Interestingly, the rest of the night was quiet. I felt comfortable trying a shift on my own after training that night.

On Sunday, I was on my own again at the assisted living facility. I was nervous, and it was a challenge going to work, but I needed to work the shift. I wasn't going to be defeated by fear. Before I left for work, I thought about how I was going to conquer my fear of PTSD, as I worked alone, and wondered what I would do if they came up. The last thing I wanted to do was call in sick again!

Then I asked Rod, "How am I going to do this?"

Rod tried to be encouraging with this PTSD issue by telling me stories, so I wouldn't think about it so hard. While they were nice stories, they really didn't do anything for me. I arrived at work and thought well, I'll see what happens.

Sunday, October 13, 2013

I went to work, and relieved the same CP as the night I had my SCAD. As we visited, I asked her the same question the other staff asked her, whether I had looked any different that night.

She said, "No, everyone kept asking me that, too. You seemed fine. I had no reason to not leave you alone! No one could believe you had a heart attack, and major procedure done that night."

As she left, she used the same words she used when she left on the night I had my heart attack, "Any questions?"

I said, laughing, "Hope not."

She said, "Call if you have any questions. I'll be up." I was relieved about that.

I started with my routine. Interestingly, I felt peaceful. I surprised myself. After that shift, I was fine, as I continued to work on my own. I made it past the hour I had my dissection, and all the way to the morning with NO ISSUES! WHEW! Reality was settling in quickly.

Bills continued to come. Every hospital trip incurred a cost. Our insurance coverage was exorbitant for us as Rod and I worked in the human services field. Thank God programs are in place to help with such enormous and unexpected bills.

Needless to say, I had to make a few phone calls to take care of the bills. The first call was to the New Ulm Medical Center. They were covered, and explained that my insurance paid it. The people to deal with the most would be the first people I needed to use which was ambulance/air services. After I heard this, I looked at the air ambulance statement, and found their phone number.

I asked, "Can you by chance find out the names of the crew who flew the helicopter that night I went to Abbott, so I could thank them."

She said, "We usually don't do that for everyone's protection, but since this case was so unique, I'll see what I could do. Somehow, I'll at least let them know how grateful you am."

How was I going to be a better person serving God at work? Well, that was ongoing training. I needed time. I remembered the lyrics I heard especially from the refrain in the song, "Shout to the Lord". Those words suggested to me how I was supposed to be a better person serving God and mankind, and they rang through me continuously. I knew I needed to serve God and His people better in ALL the areas of my life, in order to worship and Glorify God's Holy Name.

My work life was the main area in which I wanted to change something, and I did. One responsibility I wanted to decrease before my SCAD was to drop down my position with HSI. I served, as a Team Lead Assist (TLA) for HSI. The pay was pretty good, when I was offered the position, and the responsibilities weren't as great; so, taking the TLA position was financially stable.

As the Health and Human Services field constantly was refused additional state support for our company to increase wages with an additional COLA (Cost of living adjustment) for 8 years in a row, staying in that position became difficult for staff to live on with that income.

Along without an increase in wage, everyday expenses grew. Gas prices were soaring to over $4.00 per gallon, and the health insurance deductible continued to increase to one-quarter of our income before insurance companies paid anything. The rate increase for deductibles was due to government law changes, as President Obama's Affordable Care Act was enacted.

There were also fewer people to hire, as the baby boomer generation, (people born between 1959-1964, had larger families) retired. The younger generation of people accepted positions in other fields, because their wage and benefit packages were more competitive.

All those economic issues led to an increase in responsibilities for TLAs. I tried to be a team player, and stay with the position to help the company, but I had to change. The question was how?

One night, an opportunity presented itself. A woman from HSI called about my relieving her for a Sunday night shift every two weeks at this same assisted living facility. She had picked up an extra job to help with her expenses. She said the work would be in line with what I was already doing and my hours.

This coworker had thought of me, because I always asked her how it was working out there. She thought I could handle the tasks at this facility fine. I decided to try it, and thanked her for thinking of me. That's how I found the RCP position at the assisted living facility. Again, this is New Ulm; people helping people!

October 7-14, 2013

After running errands, I stopped at the HSI office. I had a work slip from the clinic and Abbott, and contacted the team leader. She had lined up a meeting for me with our Human Resources Director. I walked in, and so many people were there to see me and welcome me back. I felt relieved to see so many friendly faces, and receive so many sincere hugs.

The team leader and I went to the HR office, and I showed them the work slip. They could see my restrictions of NO appointments, shopping, or vacuuming: those duties were out. I had asked Abbott to add shoveling, as I knew that winter was coming around the corner.

I said, "I have to be at cardio rehab Mondays, Wednesdays, and Fridays at 10:00, and my cardiologist thought it would be best to start here part-time." Then I told them both that after my SCAD, "I plan to cut down, and work overnights at group homes, as soon as a position comes open." The work on the night shift would be in line with my doctor's restrictions, especially since I could sleep if everything was quiet.

Our group home was covered for sleep-night shifts. At that time, staff who had seniority could almost dictate their hours. Even though

I had seniority, I didn't want to push the other two staff members out of their positions. That's why I said *when a position comes up.*

I realized I could've taken the sleep-night hours at our site, because of my position and seniority. That decision would cost the group home two very qualified staff if I had taken their sleep-night hours. That decision would have been literally stupid and utterly selfish on my part. I believed it'd be easier for me to move to another site.

I figured the other advantage of my moving to another site was the company would have a better chance of hiring a new TLA. In the past, the TL and TLA positions filled easily, because the hours and pay were better. If I dropped down in position, the company would have more qualified people from whom to choose for a TLA. It was a risk for me dropping down in position, because of the lack of pay. I felt it was worth it, so the company would have better candidates from whom to choose.

My working at another group home was much better for everyone. They both agreed to this, and promised to keep me in mind when that type of position came open. Sleep-night positions are few and far between.

During the visit, we called the clinic to double check that it was okay with my physician to return to work, because at first, I had a difficult time finding the permission on the slip. Since I had such a difficult time finding it, I showed the other women the slip. They couldn't find it.

We called the clinic, and I told the nurse I thought Dr. Knowles put the restrictions on the work slip, but for some reason, we were having a difficult time finding it. The nurse clarified where it was on the slip. After she told us where it was, we found it, and had to laugh. After the office visit, I went back to the group home with the team leader to be acclimated to the routine, again.

Once at the group home, the team leader (TL) asked, "How did it go at the assisted living shift?"

I said, "Interestingly, it felt peaceful."

TL said, "You probably felt peaceful, because you were taken care of out there."

I thought she was right. After that comment from the TL, I knew I'd be okay working out there again.

I felt strange being back at the group home after being gone for such a long time.

TL said, "Go slow", as I was walking up the stairs.

The TL was a good friend of ours, and because of that, she picked up on the idea of the sleep-night issue I brought up at the HSI office. TL said, "Are you sure you want to go down to sleep nights, because the pay is so much less? The Team Leader Assistant [TLA] positions don't come up very often. I don't want you to make too quick of a decision, and then end up with that much less money."

I said, "I know, but after this, I really don't want the responsibilities of that position anymore. I know the sleep-nights aren't going to be open any time soon, but I want to be considered, if something comes up.

I said, "I'll have to make up the difference in pay some other way. Maybe the assisted living facility will have more hours that I can pick up. Time will tell."

The TL told me she had thought of finding extra work she could do with her HSI hours. She hadn't made an effort to do so, but was keeping her eyes open. The TL and I decided I would return in the middle part of October. That way I wouldn't arrive in the middle of the pay period for our payroll officer in Lakefield. The TL said, "Let's set you back up on the computer."

We e-mailed the payroll officer who responded right away. I knew staff in the Lakefield office had heard about my heart attack, as they donated Pay Time Off (PTO) to me when the request came out. The payroll officer was glad to hear I was well, and sent an e-mail. Her email was sweet.

The TL told me that the man who lived at the group home was difficult to handle when I was gone. I was his mainstay staff and could work with him differently than the other staff. My relationship with him was strong because I was there the most. He was as familiar with me as I was with him. While I had been gone, his next quarterly report stated that his goals went down so far because his main care provider was out on leave.

At first, I was proud that his goals went down so much, because I knew the individual needed me! But the more I thought about it, I realized how harmful that could be. What if I had died? Who would he have gone to for help? His basic needs were taken care of but that was all.

I realized that we needed to bring in new people for him now. He had to work with others to have his needs met, and to become less dependent on me. However, I'd still be there to help.

Our company thought it was a good idea to have one mainstay staff at each site, but after that, they may reevaluate that decision. After I learned about the response the individual had with other staff, I felt better about my decision to drop down from TLA to direct support professional (DSP).

The TL had me read my progress notes from the last time I was there, August 25, 2013. I thought it was weird that my writing was in his notes and then BOOM! I was out, instantly. The last entry I had written was like I was going to be at the site forever! Nothing was seen from my handwriting in his progress notes until I came back. It was FREAKY!

After completing those basics, I called it quits. That was a long enough morning for me. But another part of my plan was done: my work life. I was looking forward to going back sort of, knowing I did the right thing by dropping down to a sleep-night position. This switch of hours wasn't going to happen overnight, though. The TL wouldn't be in too much of a pickle yet.

The change was going to take time. I wasn't going to leave her or the individual high and dry, so to speak. After all, she recommended me for the TLA position, so I wanted to make sure the group home had enough staff before I moved to another site.

Plus, I wanted the right person to replace me, one to whom she and the individual could relate. Staff have their hands full working with companies who serve individuals with developmental disabilities. The work can be taxing but very rewarding. Those individuals don't ask for those disabilities; they are special people.

After I worked with those individuals and the staff for a while, I accepted all of them as part of my family. It was practically a given. Staff tended to want to make sure that everyone was well-taken care of.

Where does my changing roles at work lead to when I told God, "I could still be a better person." Well, I had wanted to switch roles with HSI and drop down to a DSP. When I met with my team leader at the group home, I was glad I told her about my decision to change positions.

The TL thought I was making too rash of a decision, and she wanted me to be sure I had made the right decision. After hearing my reasoning, again, for wanting less responsibilities and making sure everyone was taken care of, she knew I had made the right decision.

My TLA position kept me from spending as much time as I would have liked with my grandchildren who are only little once. However, helping other employers or finding other jobs to do intrigued me. I had a strong urge to work with children again. More importantly, I wanted to help more people, especially after all the prayers that were said for me from different groups of people..

Shortly after I dropped down in position with Habilitative Services Inc. (HSI), my work life changed. I maintained my full-time status with HSI as I had to have the benefits.

The assisted living facility was short staffed that year, Fall of 2013, so I worked more shifts. Those extra hours helped make up thedifference in pay I lost from going to a TLA to a direct support professional position. The extra benefit of working at the assisted living facility, was that I really enjoyed the position, staff, and residents. How can I beat that for a job?

My work life continued to change. Since I dropped down in position with HSI, I picked up hours at a new facility owned and connected with the assisted living facility where I worked. It was half an assisted a living facility and half memory care suites. Memory care differed immensely from assisted living, but I was glad to have had the opportunity to work there. It was great fun for me to meet other people, too.

Both the Catholic and public schools needed substitutes as paraprofessionals in their early childhood buildings. Even though my license had lapsed, I could sub as a teacher as well! Teaching early childhood was where I started my career in New Ulm. How interesting that my life turned itself around, and I realized what I should have been doing all along: teaching young children. I thoroughly enjoyed spending time teaching preschool.

Since I worked with all those employers, even though I had to take a decrease in pay going down in position with HSI, I actually made more money. In addition to the extra income, the work was enjoyable without all the responsibilities of the TLA position that I had held. The additional benefit was I enjoyed my position with HSI more.

I was blessed with being hired in May, 2014 as a substitute-teacher at the Head Start Migrant School in Sleepy Eye. Actually, I applied as an assistant substitute teacher, because my license had lapsed. The Center Director called and asked if I'd be interested in the teacher position.

I was surprised and delighted about this teaching offer. The Center Manager mentioned with the education and experience I had already, I'd qualify as a teacher.

I said, "Sure, I'd love to. Thanks for considering me."

She said she'd check with the Assistant Director, and set a time for an interview.

The assistant director called back that same day. We set a date for an interview later that week. The only glitch in accepting a teaching position was the limited time I had.

She said right away, "I can see you as a sub."

The Center Director agreed and she said a sub would be perfect. I said, "If it helps, I can give you my schedule, and you can put me on when you need me. If I come and you find your child count is down, I can go home. New Ulm isn't that far away."

I knew the drama of the number count at preschools from having worked at EduCare-the preschoool and daycare affiliated with the Catholic school in New Ulm, as a director; so, they were grateful for my flexibility.

I went through the training. *Time* will tell how I'm still being a better person with my employment. Because of their efforts, and the effort of the public and parochial schools, I renewed my licenses to teach. Another example of the values lived in New Ulm and the surrounding area, PEOPLE HELPING PEOPLE!

The best part of working with all those schools was the extra advantage of working with all cultures too. One thing that became apparent to me while working with different cultures was that, while we may all have different ways of living, children all grow in specific developmental stages.

That's one way I've become a better person serving God. I helped others more and worked with all ages, from the young to the old and from the neediest to the wealthiest populations in each age group.

I was glad I had decided to drop down in position with HSI. Even if it meant less income at HSI, it became a stronger way of serving God. If I dropped down in position, this would leave me with more open hours to spend time with family, especially my grandchildren.

So, one more area of my life was completed: my work life.

Now, I needed to serve God the way I should in another area: my volunteer life. I had helped with the Accelerated Reading Program (AR) within the Catholic school system for years. I had always enjoyed working with the children.

Since I had heard that the staff and children had prayed for me, I wanted more than ever to keep up with volunteering. After I arranged my work schedule, I decided to contact the AR chair to see what I could do for them.

I contacted the Catholic school's librarian to have her put my name back on the list for the AR program. She was glad to hear I was doing so well and we scheduled my return. I tired easily, so waiting to volunteer would give me another month of cardio rehab and adjust to my own health situation.

I thought the school was going to benefit from me volunteering with their reading program. But, instead, I received much more satisfaction from them. God truly works in mysterious ways.

One Friday, I arrived early to be updated on how to run the computers, etc. The librarian and I talked about my situation, and she said, "You know, I think one of our volunteers' mom had that same condition. Her dissection was a while ago, but her son's here today, volunteering, and we should ask him. They are fairly new to the community. I think it'd be great for you two to meet if you're interested."

I was all in for that. Meeting another person with the same condition I had, SCAD, right in New Ulm! Not that the illness was good, of course, but the support was.

A few minutes later, he came and I met him.

He said, "Oh, I'm sure Mom would love to meet you!" I offered him my number. "You can give this to her, and she can call me if she feels like it. It'd be great to have the support."

He said, "I'll do that right away!"

With that, the children started coming in, and we needed to go back to work! That was partly why I received more satisfaction volunteering for the program than the program gained from my volunteering.

The other part I gained satisfaction from volunteering with the reading program is the kids. Kids can say the darnedest things! I remember another volunteer, Vicky, was helping a child on a test question.

The student was having some difficultly reading, and she was trying to help him with the words, and figure out the answer. The child was stumped about an answer on the test at one point and finally confessed, "I don't know that (answer) one. My mom had me skip reading that part!"

We all burst out laughing, and he laughed, too.

The volunteer said, "Well, you tell your mom she can't do that anymore!"

Be careful, moms. You are accountable too!

Since the personal/volunteering area of my life was settled, another aspect of my life needed work. I had to organize my personal area.

Now that I felt more independent being able to drive, the next big part of my life was going back to my personal area! That was a big part because it included going back to having coffee.

Yep, my friend and I had been going for years to Perkins since we met back in the later 1990s. We decided to meet once a week, as long as we could, as a stress-relief break from life.

Through the years and lots of coffee, we had seen kids graduate, marry, and have children of their own. Additionally, we both became grandparents! Interestingly, the now-grown kids sometimes came.

They came the first time Linda and I resumed our stress-relief break after my heart attack! Everyone gave hugs. It was nice to have the group back together.

Our server who usually waits on us stopped me, and said she had read my thankyou letter in the paper. She said she was shocked but glad to see I was okay. Now, she looks ahead to help us if we have trouble ordering something with a low salt intake. What a lovely woman! Who else would take the time to do that extra step for the health of a person!

Eating establishments could have their own slogans of 500ca/500mg salt as a PR thing. It would be great to include the salt intake in their menus. That practice would make it much easier for heart patients to choose meals and with less hassle for the poor servers as they wouldn't have to keep asking the cooks about the salt content in meals.

The best aspect I appreciated about my coffee friend was that she had been through so much that nothing shocked her. Since her husband was instrumental in changing the course of our remodeling project, they, too, received a thank you with a letter.

I asked her what she thought about it. She said, "It was great and so moving. I had everyone read it. When I showed it to my husband, he said, 'Leave it to her, out of all of us, to get to meet God.'"

I asked, "How did you find out about my heart attack?"

I discovered their son and our daughter were social media friends. Their son shared the information with his parents as soon as he learned of my plight.

The next week, she and I met alone at our favorite restaurant. I asked her more in depth about how she found out?

She said, "When I heard it was you, I asked God right away not to take you away from me yet. After I prayed for you, I heard someone or something telling me they were going to take you for just a little while!" After Linda heard that, she felt better about the results of m heart attack.

She added, "One night, when I was sleeping, and

you came to me, and you were really mad that you didn't have your coffee."

I laughed and said, "That's funny because I remember thinking at one point when I was out, how is my friend going to find out I can't make it to coffee today?"

We both laughed at that. It was a relief knowing not only that she wasn't waiting forever for me and more importantly, she believed me!

After my friend left, I recognized a couple I had seen in church. I decided to introduce myself, and we struck up a conversation. In the process of a two-hour conversation with them. Imagine a two-hour conversation with a couple you had never met. I told them about my heart attack and Near-Death Experience.

We had talked about serious health issues, so that was why I had decided to tell them about my experience. I mentioned how, as we descended into Minneapolis, I had thought "Well, whatever's going to happen, is going to happen now, and I hope I did some good.

The gentleman said right away, "You released yourself and were ready to go." That statement made a profound impact on me, especially coming from somebody I had just met. They wanted a copy of my letter, so I e-mailed it to them.

They and others think my letter still should be published somewhere, but we don't know where. We still visit with each other and have great conversations! They had no doubt that what I had was a Near-Death Experience. They had just met me and never doubted me for a moment! To this date, they are among my biggest fans with this project. They still ask for permission to send out copies. Others still encourage me to finish my story, and another friend is helping me, too.

Also, with family, we celebrated our wedding anniversary. The evening was incredible.

In my personal/recreation life, one thing I decided to do was to quit drinking. Basically, my decision was because of my meds, but it was also a personal decision. I told God I could still be a better person doing that, so kept up with it. After all, my cardio rehab nurse said meds and doctors could only do so much.

Along with family, in my personal life, I worked on building my piano skills again. Some days, I did quite well scheduling that, and sometimes it took me a couple of days before I played again.

I learned to play the song I heard when I was with God: *Shout to the Lord.* I am pretty good after many hours of practicing. I laminated and learned other pieces that I always said I wanted to play.

Since I practiced more, I seemed to pick up on new pieces more easily. AMAZING! I'm not sure why I started playing more, but it relieved my stress after long days at work.

Of course, in my personal life, since God said it was okay, I continued to be a big Packer fan! We often went to the bowling alley to watch them when they played at the same time as the Vikes. If I could watch them at home, I watched them in my porch. I decorated it in green and gold with lots of Packer stuff.

Recently, as I looked around the porch, I thought something was missing. I couldn't figure out what it was. I started thinking about the values of the Packer team again: God, family, the Green Bay Packers. As I remembered those values, that nagging feeling of what was missing came: a crucifix!

Yep, that's what I needed. The crucifix would keep me focused on why I watched the game and continued to be such a fan but not just any fan. God told me I needed to be a good one. Spending time in my personal life with my own interests was how I was still being a better person.

After having my personal life more together, I started doing more housework and running errands on my own. It helped that cardio rehab was underway. That gave me the energy I needed.

After my driving lessons with Rod and Rose, I had to learn to be more secure about driving alone. The trip for coffee and cardio rehab were my first short trips driving on my own. Since I felt okay to drive, I was compelled to have more of a routine life, a new norm so-to-speak. I was determined to do the driving on my own and even though I was edgy about that, I had to start sometime. Driving to cardio rehab and Perkins on my own was a good start.

I needed to continue with cardio rehab. At the same time, I tried to live by the answer I found in those lyrics to the song I heard when I was with God and to the response I had given to God.

Chapter 23:

Back to Cardio Rehab 3

By the end of September, 2013, I participated more in adding my input during conversations with the staff and other cardio rehab patients there. I didn't participate in the conversations, at first, because I was irritated with myself, thinking I had caused my SCAD, and put my soul into grave danger concerning my afterlife. Now that I knew my SCAD truly wasn't my fault, after participating in conversations with the stem cell research doctor about the facts that cardiologists can't predict or prevent SCAD, I felt reassured about myself.

I also felt healthier. Plus, I was at cardio rehab so long and with this team, it became a natural process to jump into conversations whether I wanted to or not. The team was pretty good about forcing the issue, too, as they asked personal questions that only I could answer.

The main reason for wanting to become stronger was, of course, I had the answer to the response I gave to God on how I was going to still be a better person, and how I wanted to fulfill this answer in ALL the areas of my life! I was determined now to get well, and do what I was called upon to do.

At the beginning of October, I drove to cardio rehab and felt more independent. On the way to cardio rehab, I met one of our neighbors who worked at the New Ulm Medical Center. He said he had seen my Letter to the Editor via the Medical Center's Marketing/Communications Specialist who e-mailed it to everyone at the center. He said he had read the e-mail and brought it home to his wife.

I was surprised that so many people had read the letter. I thanked him for letting me know. I told this neighbor I was on my way to cardio rehab, and didn't want to keep them waiting. Then, we vowed to arrange for another neighborhood night out rally!

That same day, the Allina Communication Specialist came to cardio rehab to take pictures she needed, so the story could be written for the Health Edition in the New Ulm Journal. She said, "Someone from the Journal will be calling you, as well.

Kitty added, "I'll try to contact Dr. Rayl about meeting with you. I tried before I came, but couldn't reach him. He's hard to contact because I saw his schedule, and he's usually the night ER doctor. I'll do what I can, though."

I had hoped to thank and meet him. Of course, I had met him already, but didn't know who he was that morning. I figured I'd think of another way to thank him.

The interview personnel called and we talked mostly by phone, because it was easier to do than meet somewhere else. I was given the part of the copy that concerned me for my approval. I learned that my story was going to be published in the November 18 issue of the Health Edition of the New Ulm Journal.

In Dr. Rayl's part of the interview, I saw for the first time that the word *dying* was, from a medical perspective, connected with my condition. That was the eye-opening proof for me that convinced me that my visit with God was a Near-Death Experience. A doctor had used the phrase that I had been dying, finally, confirmation that I was dead!

I had forgotten what kind of progress I had made in cardio rehab. The cardio rehab team bragged about my success at the end of the fourth week. I thought my progress couldn't be that big of a deal. When I saw the results on the computer screen though, I could actually see how I gradually improved.

I understood the process of my wellness now, but I still didn't believe my progress was as big as a deal as they made it out to be. My progress became a big deal to me the more I thought about it. After all, when I started I was in a wheel chair being pushed by my daughter. By early October, I could drive and walk all on my own!

Those accomplishments were achieved, because of the advantage of cardio rehab, I hated to admit that. I remembered participating in the program because I was supposed to, thinking that it wouldn't do me any good whatsoever.

Around the fourth week of cardio rehab October 2013, a nice addition to the group appeared. He was all dressed in green and gold attire from top to bottom. Yes, another Packer fan joined us. The cardio rehab team said this was unusual that two Packer fans were ever in the same session. I wore a Packer sweatshirt so we really had a good time, and talked about our team. The Packers weren't having a very good year as our quarterback, Aaron Rodgers, was injured and out for six weeks.

Everyone always thought I had a *knack* when it came to predicting the plays of the game. More often than not, my predictions came out right, whether it'd be the call of the play, result of the play or ending (even if the Pack lost). My predictions were uncanny. But as a Packer fan, it was part of my soul.

By the second time, Minnesota and Green Bay played that year, my prediction in cardio rehab was that the game was going to be a tie. Both teams were playing at the same level, and the results weren't very good. Nobody would agree with me with that prediction, as a tie happened only about six times or so in the history of the sport between the two teams.

In the end, I was right! It was a tie game. Everybody was very quiet that Monday morning after the game. Athey couldn't imagine how my prediction of a tie game came true.

Before my visit with God, I might have harassed a few fans and told them, "I told you so," but I remembered again what God said **about having to be a good Packer fan.** I decided to say nothing about the game. Our other Packer fan did too. Teasing other Viking fans wouldn't have done any good for anyone anyway. Now I understand what God said about being a "good Packer fan".

Instead of harassing the Viking fans now, the other Packer fan, and I had great conversations of Wisconsin, where we were from, and what brought us to New Ulm! He was an employee at the college here. He was older, and we understood very well whose turf we were on. We weren't in the market of making people feel bad. The staff and other patients' expressions on their faces after my prediction said it all. How nice to have a Wisconsin synod college in New Ulm, Minnesota! Packer support!

In the middle of November, I ended my cardio rehab sessions. Evidently, it didn't matter if I was well enough to be done. That was all the sessions for which the insurance company paid!

IN MY OPINION… Little do those insurance companies know. If they let people stay in cardio rehab until patients reached up to 5 METS, which is what cardiologists recommend, they would save more money than they think. Patients would have fewer recurring heart attacks if they reach up to 5 METS! But what do cardiologists know? According to insurance companies, wellness boils down to the almighty dollar!

On the last day of my sessions, the article on me came out in the Journal. Everyone thought it was great, and I hadn't even read it yet. A staff person whom I didn't know came in from another department, and said he thought it was great! He didn't introduce himself, so for all I know, he could have been Dr. Rayl himself.

I didn't remember Dr. Rayl from my fateful morning, so I still had no idea what he looked like: the mysterious Dr. Rayl! One day, we may meet. After all this time, I still wanted to know what happened in that emergency room.

Even though I didn't *technically have a name for* what I had experienced, *My Visit with God* was well accepted. I believe it was well-accepted because around that time, several books on life-after-life started to be written.

After my article came out, a friend from HSI sent a card and called. She gave me a book she had read about Near-Death Experiences.

Another friend from Sleepy Eye, had read my story in the paper. She stopped over with a card and a book. I was at work, but Rod said she visited for an hour. A friend we met through my sister, Jill, sent a card with a gift of money. She and her husband were the first couple we met when Rod and I moved to New Ulm.

I believe those books on Near-Death Experiences were all given to me after people had received my letter, which was God's way of saying, "Yes, Jean, this is what you had: a Near- Death Experience. Your visit with Me was REAL. Wake up and share your story."

At the end of cardio rehab, I was graded to see if I was ready to graduate! According to the heart monitor, and the METS on the machines, it was showing that I was up to 5 METS. I had met the criteria and was ready to graduate! Now, I had a chance to win a prize!

The head nurse in cardio rehab pulled out a little box for me, and started the prize up. I looked forward to something big, as I remember Rod earned a t-shirt when he graduated from cardio rehab. When Clarice showed me that little prize, I looked at it and read Allina Health.

I asked, "What is it?"

She said, "It's a pedometer."

I said, "What? A pedometer? That's it? I wanted a t-shirt!"

We laughed and she showed me how it worked. The pedometer was interesting, and proved more effective than I had thought! I found out from using the pedometer, that when I worked at HSI, I walk around 1,500 steps; at Woodstone, 3,000 steps; and at the assisted living facility, I walked 5,000 steps! The pedometer was definitely more useful than a t-shirt!

I thought that was the end of my story, but that was when my article in the Journal came out. More media and prayers continued to circulate, and I still couldn't figure out what I had done to deserve all those prayers. So much good came out of a little thank you, a simple act that seemed to be a lost art today!

Little did I know what was to develop from the media! The media could be a good source of news. The success of my story made me wonder why the media didn't want to publish more good stories like that. At this time, the media aired stories of sex-abuse scandals, school shootings, murder. It seemed as nothing good in the world happened. People told me they didn't want to hear the news stories anymore.

People need to tell their stories and share their experiences, especially the GOOD SIDE! That side always seemed to be covered up. The goodness keeps us connected.

My ECHO after cardio rehab was done, and I thought my jobs were finished. My thank you was written in the Journal for the New Ulm Medical Center and the community. I was well enough after stem-cell research and cardio rehab to move on with the answer to how I was going to still be a better person in ALL the other areas of my life. I was still grateful for all the prayers that people had said for me. I wanted to do more for everyone.

The results of my ECHO were sent to Dr. Knowles, my primary physician. A couple days later Dr. Knowles' office called. They told me that my ECHO changed but it wasn't significant so they didn't warrant any further testing.

Those results had me worried, because any change to me was significant. Dr. Knowles' office said they would send the results to my cardiologist at Abbott, and he would call me if necessary. I was to make an appointment with him for the next time Dr. Traverse was in New Ulm.

In January, I would have an idea what Dr. Knowles' office meant regarding the results of my ECHO. I made an appointment then to see

Dr. Traverse. Little did I know how significant this next appointment with him was going to be.

I thought my physical self was well, but that was about to change. Curves had decided to close. We had been a close-knit group of ladies and were saddened by Curves' closing, but we certainly understood the issue. We had one last potluck at Curves so everyone could say goodbye. I was glad because I had started going back after I had completed cardio rehab in order to keep up with a workout, and I hadn't seen all of our Curves' friends yet.

Interestingly, at the potluck, one members' husband was a doctor at the New Ulm Medical Center. When she heard my story, she said, "Jean, I think I know the other lady who had that same condition. She goes to our church. Do you know her?"

I said, "No, but I'm hoping to meet her. Will you take my name and number and then give them to her? It would be great if we could meet."

She said, "Sure. I should see her sometime this week."

I gave her my number to give to that SCAD lady and left it at that. That act of kindness made me once again aware of the beauty and charm of New Ulm: very generational and people helping people.

My Near-Death Experience was beautifully designed from Heaven (as I know everything is). I couldn't argue. I forgot how all of life was designed from God in Heaven. When this happened, it snapped me back in reality: Fast!

I BELIEVED I was in control of my life's decisions, but I was not. I REALIZED I WAS ONLY GUARANTEED THE BREATH I WAS TAKING! God was in control! I was where I was because God wanted me there! That was the bottom line! GOD WAS IN CONTROL!

That year, the holidays were more important to me than ever. Somehow, I wanted to thank everyone for all they had done for me. I wanted to do something extra for everyone that year. The holidays were my favorite time of the year, and represented another chance to be thankful for what everyone had done for me.

CHAPTER 24:

THE HOLIDAYS

THANKSGIVING, 2013, I continued to have requests for *My Visit with God* letter. I was so appreciative of what everyone had done for me, and I wanted to do something special for everyone for the holidays. Thanksgiving, as usual, was spent at my sister's home in LaCrosse. Many immediate and extended family members were there.

They asked how I was doing and told me I looked great! They had prayed for me, too. Most of us went to Sunday Mass. After Mass, the priest said, "Go in peace to Glorify God by your life, which is relatively new." I had wondered if priests said that in LaCrosse, like they did in New Ulm. I thought maybe the Blessing at the end of Mass was only a New Ulm saying, so I paid particular attention to it at the end of Mass. I discovered the blessing was the same in LaCrosse.

I decided that had to be the answer to how I was going to be a better person for God. The priests state it at the end of every Mass. After all this time, I had only begun to hear it New Ulm after returning from Abbott with a major life-threatening condition. I realized that was the answer to God's question that He had for me.

As we dressed for the weather and packed to go home, my sister< Nancy told me about the client she was with when my call came about my emergency. He happened to be an ER doctor.

My sister said, "Jean, the ER doctor I was with when the call came about you still wanted to talk to you about what you saw on the other side. When the call came, he looked right at me."

He said, "Nancy, when she wakes up, I want to know what she saw on the other side!'"

Nancy explained that he had been an ER doctor for more than 30 years and obviously had experienced those issues in his practice. She said, "I gave him the strangest look, because I didn't know what he was talking about when he said the other side, but I said, "Okay, so I could leave our meeting."

I said, "How did he know I was going to go to the other side (wanting to use his terminology because I didn't know what religion he was)?"

Nancy said, "Because you were shocked!"

I thought, That's how he knew I was going to go to the other side?

That ER doctor didn't know me from Adam, but he knew I was going to cross over. I was amazed that a total stranger knew I was going to have that experience: a total stranger!

I wrote down some other things that had happened to me, using Nancy's copy of my Visit with God letter. I mentioned the clouds, the shape they were in, how I was alone, and a few other details. We never met, but maybe one day we will. ER doctors are incredible people. They have to think fast and on-the-run to save lives. They are truly a gift from God.

After Thanksgiving, I wanted to do something more for my family, who had said prayers and sent cards and letters. I decided I would do something extra for everyone at Christmas.

Christmas 2013 arrived. I wrote my Christmas letter and answered God's question for me, "What are you going to do for me?"

While I prepared for Christmas, I bought candy baskets for the two classes at St Anthony's who prayed for me. For the older class, I specifically mentioned how my test scores improved, and how I didn't need any further stem cell infusions because they had continued to say prayers for me. I figured they could handle this information because of the age the kids were. I wrote down the scores of my tests and explained how they were just barely above the criteria to disqualify me for the infusion.

Our oldest grandchild's class was given a basket, too. They had said prayers for me, and I thought they should have one. They enjoyed receiving the candy. It was a special day for our oldest grandchild when that happened.

Yes, I thought sending those baskets was one way to thank those classes for praying for me. However, I was proven wrong again. The two classes sent thankyous to me which were the best thankyous I ever received. They were handwritten and colored and each signed their own name.

I started buying baskets for one or two groups for the two classes at St Anthony's who prayed for me, and ended up sending out 10.

Our family met in the Cities as usual at my sisters' houses for Christmas. Everyone came for a few hours at least before taking off to other families and vacation spots. Life went on. That was far enough for me to venture. I was better at going places, especially after the trip to LaCrosse at Thanksgiving, but traveling to the Cities was far enough for me at Christmas.

I always felt better being home. I was never much of a traveler. Traveling was always exhausting for me, and that's why I like to be a stay-at-home kind of person!

While we were in the Cities for Christmas, Dad said to me, "You are going to do something GREAT!"

I didn't know what that greatness was yet, but to me if I could get to Heaven, that would be GREAT enough for me! After all, I thought, I'm just me, a Catholic-born, Wisconsin-native, German, Irish, Swiss, Luxembourger, Green Bay Packer fan. I'm one person who doesn't have clout (according to worldly ideas), or status, or lots of material things: just me! That's it. I don't know that I'll ever do anything GREAT like Dad said, but it's a compliment! On top of my spouse, my parents are the people of whom every child wants them to be proud!

I thought I thanked everyone for their prayers through the gifts I gave at Christmas, but I was wrong, again! Instead, the best gifts, it turned out were ones I received.

Even though I couldn't keep working on my story due to life routine issues, I worked to put the answer to my response that I could still be a better person to God's question into practice, in all the areas of my life. That wasn't as easy as I thought. Instead of being accomplished overnight, putting my answer into practice, was going to take a commodity we believe we have, until all of a sudden, we do not: **Time.**

CHAPTER 25:

TIME

I'M ITALICIZING the word *time* throughout the rest of the book to help me remember what little of it I have. Every community seems to have a structure that *re*presents *time*. In New Ulm, the city has a monument called the Glockenspiel. It shows the different groups of peopleinvolved in establishing New Ulm, Minnesota. The Glockenspiel shows what the city's values are to help people grow both spiritually and physically.

Donations of *time,* effort, and money from local contributors were joined by donors from foreign countries and Minnesota cities to complete the structure. That clock represents the spiritual and physical values of the people of New Ulm.

People seem to think *time* is guaranteed. People plan vacations, life events and holidays believing they are going to be there. People forget how truly priceless *time* is until they realize nothing is guaranteed: especially *time* .

I should've realized the answer to God's question, **"What are you going to do for me?"** The answer was represented in the Glockenspiel. The Glockenspiel has 12 figurines that represent the German culture and all the sectors of life New Ulm has to offer its people to ensure the spiritual and physical growth of the whole person. One of the figurines is a pastor portrayed as reading from the Bible.

Around January, 2014, after I finished with cardio rehab and the holidays, I had arranged a routine of sorts that coincided with my work limits after approval from Dr. Traverse. I was ready and well enough to put my foolproof plan in effect to account for all the areas in my life, or so I thought.

This became my for-sure-fire plan. My schedule, for instance, in a day was 8 hours of work, 8 hours of sleep, 2 hours for meal prep and meal. Out of 24 hours in a day, that time accounted for 18 of those hours which left a total of 6 hours in each day. Each grandchild was going to have one hour of my undivided attention. That left 4 hours. One hour was designated for prayer and one hour for a nap. That left me with 2 hours. One of those hours was going to be for housework, and the other hour was for Rod. That schedule accounted for 24 hours in my day. My day was full and ALL the areas of my life were accounted for. That was my foolproof plan by which I would try to live. That was in accord with the answer I gave to God.

My plan to schedule all the areas of my life in a day fell apart immediately because Louise and Bruce traveled with the girls to Guatemala to work at the church's mission in the winter of 2014. The mission was supported by Bruce's grandparents back in the day.

I was disappointed with their trip, because my schedule didn't account for it. I wondered how I would have *time* with the grandchildren each day if they were in Guatemala!

I thought of every possible reason for Louise and Bruce to leave the girls with me, but that didn't work. I had to accept that they were the parents, and it was their choice what to do with their children. I figured I'd make up the difference in *time* when they came back.

The worst part was I realized that our grandchildren didn't need their Grandma Jean as much as I thought. That was difficult to accept. I was afraid I might die again, since I thought I had given the wrong response to God's question about my grandchildren needing their Grandma Jean. They were the reason I asked for my physical self back. I wondered why on earth did I have another chance to keep my earthly body? I decided our grandchildren must need to find their own path to Heaven. Embarrassingly, I needed to come to terms with the fact that our grandchildren would be okay living without me.

I needed to face the reality that our grandchildren would be fine without their Grandma Jean. The truth was, I needed them more to keep my earthly body rather the fact that they needed me to live. They had their parents who would meet their needs. They may be sad if I died, but they would move on with their lives, so they could go to Heaven.

I realized life would go on without me. So, from here on, I would live by the answer I gave God: I could still be a better person in all areas of my life!

Since our grandchildren were going to be gone, I had two extra hours in each day. Since I needed more training at work at the new site, I thought I'd fill in the extra two hours with training. The extra *time* at the new site would allow me to train faster to help cover hours.

Our TL resigned to accept a position with HSI in a mentor role while working at her new employment. I had thought my work plan was in place, but this area was changing, too. Since our TL had resigned, the TL position at our old site was given to me… I accepted very reluctantly. *That wasn't part of my plan! I wanted to go down in position, not up!*

The company had such a staff shortage, there wasn't anyone else management would be comfortable giving that position to on such short notice. I continued to work as a temporary team leader at the old site knowing the company would specifically hire a team leader for that site first.

Instead of my extra *time* being spent at the new site which I thought was where the two extra hours were going to be used for, I spent them at the old site while still being trained at the new one. Yeah, my work area changed! Not only that, as I mentioned I went up in position, not down! That was not how I planned it, but how God did!

I had one benefit of having the temporary team leader position. The benefit was that this role made me realize I wanted to drop down in position, more than ever! We had four and a half staff and our lifestyle specialist, to cover a house 24/7. Our life-style specialist was willing to cover shifts only if needed!

My concerns resurfaced. Who could I call for help? Whathappened if I or anyone else were sick? What would happen if people couldn't come in for their shifts due to the weather? That position would interfere with my foolproof plan of accounting for all the areas in my life!

More concerns continued; my mind raced. How could I fulfill the answer I came up with for God: that I could still be a better person. That wouldn't work if I were filling in with the role of team leader, which would take up more *time*. I kept going back and forth with that question. I was afraid God might take me again if I couldn't be a better person in all areas of my life!

I wanted to serve HSI, because they had always been good to Rod and me, no matter what. The hiring staff for team leaders knew my concerns and worked hard to fill my team leader position at our site, first. That winter we lost four team leaders *at one time* and our lifestyles specialist who had taken a new position and had two weeks left. Those were big positions to fill as three of four of thoseemployees had worked for HSI for over ten years. We had all thought they would be at HSI **FOREVER.**

I decided to shop myself for my clients because I had no other option. I survived most of the winter months. I shopped a little *at a time* and made several trips to buy what the individuals needed. That shopping plan worked. HSI realized they needed to hire a new team leader for our site quickly, because little did any of us know what was about to happen next.

January, 2014, proved to be a very cold winter. We'd had many snowstorms already and everyone was exhausted. I had taken one of the guys to an appointment January 21 (a restriction I wasn't supposed to do because of the risk of being exposed to too many germs). Since no team leader had been hired yet, I didn't have a choice.

I felt tired and had a headache I couldn't shake the morning of those appointments. Those feelings weren't unusual for me as winter is usually a difficult season for me to handle. The trip went fine. I finished my 3-10 shift and went home to bed.

On January 22, I worked the morning shift. Two individuals lived at the house now. The other individual had an appointment at the clinic that morning. Once again, no one else could take him but me.

I had that headache, struggled, but made the appointment. I drove home around 11:00 and went right to bed. I had a staff meeting at 1:00 that afternoon.

I was late to the staff meeting after my nap as I had to make several trips to the bathroom. During the staff meeting, I had to leave because diarrhea hit me so quickly, I couldn't even make it to the bathroom at the HSI office. I was too embarrassed to say anything about being sick.

While looking at our Lifestyle Specialist, I said, "I'm sorry. I have to go. I don't feel well."

Our Lifestyle Specialist knew of my earlier heart condition. She thought I wasn't feeling well from that vs. the diarrhea I had. She told me I could leave. I drove home, ran to the bathroom, and started vomiting profusely. Post-traumatic stress disorder (PTSD) settled in, and I was terrified! I tried calling Rod. He didn't answer (I should be used to that by now).

The *time* was around 2:30 pm. I knew Louise would be picking up our grandchild from school. I called her and left a message to see if she'd come, stay with me, and pick up some flu medicine. She didn't answer. I thought she was probably there. I called the school and the Office Manager answered.

I said, "Hi. This is Jean Nielsen. Is Louise there yet? I'm not feeling well, and want to see if she could pick up some meds for me after she picks up Lola."

The Office Manager said, "Oh, let me see. I'll try to find her."

A couple minutes later, the school's Office Manager called back and Rod answered. She told him what was going on and that Louise didn't come since Lola had been sick. Rod told her he was home so not to worry about it. He picked up some meds for me, and I stayed in bed for a couple days.

On January 25, I was still sick. I made an appointment to see one of the doctors. My doctor wasn't in, but her husband was. I made an appointment with him since he knew my history, and I didn't want to explain my issues to a new physician at that point.

The exam was embarrassing as I ended up pretty sick. Thankfully, the nurse was kind and thoughtful. She said, "Jean do you want to lie down?"

I said, "Yeah. I'd better."

I sat up on the table, she grabbed a blanket and basin for me, and I rested.

She said, "I'll find your doctor right away. He has an intern, and would it be okay if he brings her?"

At first, I thought I didn't want the intern because I was sick. Then it dawned on me that that's why they're here: to learn and to deal with sick people, so I agreed.

The doctor came in with the intern. He explained to the intern about my heart condition last fall, and that the SCAD, and my procedure had never before been done with someone surviving. He made one key point to the intern.

He said, "She had a visit with God."

I was impressed that he told his intern about my visit with God. I could tell the intern was surprised at the comment concerning my visit with God as she gave the doctor a quizzical look, like she thought I was a nut. He confirmed my experience by nodding yes to her so she knew my visit with God was REAL!

After testing, he discovered that I had Influenza B. Yep, that quickly. The doctor decided to put me in the ER for fluids and antinausea meds, because of the sensitivity of my dissection. He stressed that I wouldn't have to even see a doctor!

I thought whew that was the last thing I wanted to do was go back see a doctor, and experience another trip to Abbott (even though I was very appreciative of what they'd done for me). The doctor anticipated my fear of going back to Abbott, and that's why he stressed the NO DOCTOR visit. I appreciated that!

He continued, "If you aren't feeling better, you could stay for the night, but you can make that decision after you have meds."

His nurse wheeled me into the ER, and the nurses hooked me up to IVs. Some of them had seen my story and told me how nice it was.

I said, "You guys deserve it. You really don't get enough credit!"

I don't know what meds they put in the IV's, but I slept until 3:00.

I felt much better. Rod picked up more meds then came for me.

People talk about Post Traumatic Stress Disorders-PTSD after major life crisis issues. I'm not a big believer in PTSD, especially because I thought if I would've had an issue with it, it would've happened on my first shift back to work, but that went fine.

The PSTD Fear happened when I started to become sick, especially, because there wasn't any one to contact. Interestingly, at the New Ulm Medical Center Emergency Room, I felt safe because I knew first-hand that I was well-taken care of before, and **OUR DOCTORS DO KNOW WHAT THEY'RE DOING!**

I should've known I could handle the flu situation on my own. God had me have my SCAD at work where I was alone. I believe part of having my SCAD at work was to prove to myself I could handle more things on my own than I believed. But when situations come up so quickly, I don't always think fast on my feet.

A few psychologist friends and friends of mine said maybe I was nervous and scared since it was the first time I had been sick after my dissection. All I know was that I was grateful I was at the New Ulm Medical Center!

After the hospital visit, I recuperated quickly and was back to a normal routine in a couple days. After I had the flu for four days, the wellness area of my life threw me off my foolproof plan. I couldn't figure out how to make up the difference I missed with the other areas of my life when all I could do then was take care of my physical health.

Being stubborn as is the nature of both the German and Irish ethnic groups, I tried to start over again with my foolproof master plan to account for all the areas of my life in a day. I believed that was the answer to Gods' question as to how I was going to be a better person: to have all the areas of my life accounted for in a day.

However, little did I know that my foolproof plan was going to be interrupted again until after my appointment *time* in February with Dr. Traverse. I decided to take care of my physical health then make up for the rest of the *time* in all the areas of my life, later, and then FOR-SURE, I would account for fulfilling the answer to God's question. My physical self was going to be taken care of with help.

CHAPTER 26:

STEM CELL RESEARCH PART 2

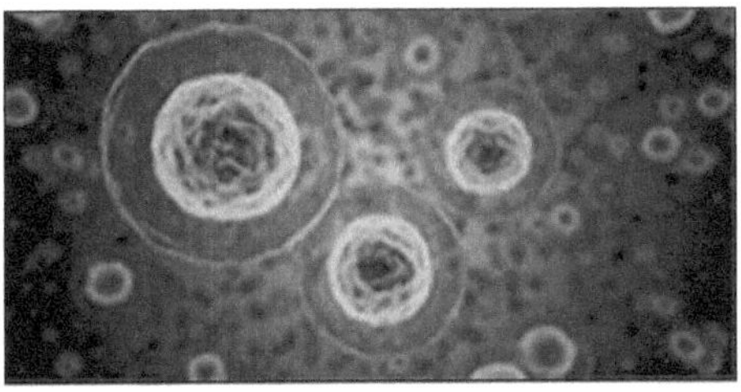

FEBRUARY 2014 was here and after I was well enough from the flu, I made an appointment to see my cardiologist, Dr. Traverse, who was going to be in New Ulm. He noticed my ECHO had changed. Dr. Traverse asked, "Would you be interested to see if you qualified for the same Stem Cell Research Study you participated in last September? Your ECHO has changed. Only this time, the study would be for the randomized part of the study not for the Safety part. The randomized part of the All Star Study means you would have the possibility of receiving a placebo instead of real stem cells." I asked, "Can I have the tests in New Ulm?"

Dr. Traverse said, "No. All the tests have to be done at Abbott." Reluctantly, as I didn't want to drive up to the Cities myself, I said,

"Well, sure… if it helps."

I became anxious and nervous, but I wanted to see the difference in the results of my ECHO. I didn't spend too much time being nervous, as I had been involved in the last study. I knew I had a distinct possibility of being disqualified. I decided to quit worrying about it and would do what I had done before: participate in the study and let God call the shots. If I was meant to have the infusion, the tests would prove that. Also, qualifying for the stem cells would be God's choice, as everything is, not mine. I was beginning to understand the saying, "God is in control!"

Dr. Traverse said, "We can use heart attack patients up to a year after their heart attacks."

I knew how much PTO I had left and said, "Okay. Do I contact Jane again?"

Dr. Traverse said, "Yes. I'll have her contact you, and you two can set up a time for the testing again."

I contacted Jane, and she had already sent me an e-mail and left a message. The next day, I called Jane, and we visited. She explained the study again and emphasized the fact that this was the randomized phase of the study. However, the participants in the randomized phase favored recipients receiving actual stem cells by a two-thirds chance, which made me feel better.

Jane said, "It was interesting. I had just opened your case again, and wondered what could we do for you? As soon as I thought that, the call from Dr. Traverse came. He said he had just seen you and that you wanted to try again since your ECHO had changed.'"

Jane checked with the research people who cleared my case again for participating. After my case was cleared, we made an appointment for late March. Then, Jane learned Dr. Henry was coming back, and going to be in the clinic on the first Wednesday in April.

Jane called me back when she found this out. Jane said, "Jean. I just found out Dr. Henry is going to be here in April. I thought you might like to see him if you can, by any chance, take that day off."

Of course, I jumped at the chance to see Dr. Henry again. By the grace of God, I was granted the day off. I thought Rose would appreciate meeting Dr. Henry, since she was the first one at Abbott that crazy morning! I called her, and, with God's help, she was given that time off work, too.

Remodeling the physical part of a person comes in many ways. My physical self was being remodeled with the stem cell research underway. Little did I know I was going to be remodeling more than only my physical body.

Chapter 27:

Remodeling

Ah, Winter 2014: another cold winter indeed. Why do I live in Minnesota? But, Minnesotans deal with the cold because that's what we do.

As one of the nurses at Abbott stated, "Who doesn't want to live in Minnesota?"

I have to remind myself of that every winter!

Yes, the physical self of a person changes in many ways. Now that the Stem Cell Research II process was arranged for my physical body, another part of my physical self that needed to be dealt with was our physical house.

Before my SCAD, Rod and I decided to remodel the house. We had wanted the change in case we ever had to sell it, FAST! I started to reline up things for remodeling our basement.

With the help of our local businesses, Klossner Construction, Puhlmann Lumber, Schulz Plumbing, Paul's Electric and Treat's Carpeting, everything was ready to go and materials ordered, and were stored at their expense. Those businesses didn't expect payment yet.

All of those local businesses were going to wait until the project was completed before Rod and I needed to pay them! We hired all of them before, so I reasoned they figured we were reliable to pay them when they finished. All we were waiting for was *time.*

All those businesses also gave us ideas on how to SAVE money! I don't believe larger businesses in larger cities would have given us ideas to SAVE money! They told us of only the projects that needed to be done, that's it!

I thought about thanking those businesses, because of their honesty and integrity of waiting for the project to be finished before expecting payment. I didn't know how, but I was going to give them a really big thank you. I figured I had *time* to do that; thank them! Little did I know, I was going to receive a greater thank you from them, than any thank you I could've come up with to give them!

When Louise called them about my SCAD, they all STOPPED PRODUCTION! They didn't expect payment, and were willing to wait for the start of the project and payment until I was ready, even though they had ordered the supplies they needed, and stored them at their expense!

How could I ever come up with a thank you big enough to show them how I appreciated that? Another example of the values people in New Ulm, Minnesota live by; PEOPLE HELPING PEOPLE!

We had our neighbor, Dave refinish the floors, and now the rest of the house needed to be completed. When our physical house was finished, I could continue keeping the promise I made to God!

The finished remodeling project was a relief. Now, for sure, if we ever had to sell, the house would sell fast, because all the rooms inside and outside were done! Plus, even if we didn't sell, by having thehouse remodeled, we'd never have to do another remodeling project EVER! The remodeled house was a win-win situation for us.

Now that the home remodeling project was completed, I was going to account for how I was going to be a better person in all the areas of my life for God. Just as I thought the work area of my life was taken care of with (HSI), another transition with work was in the works.

Chapter 28:

More Work Changes

God works in mysterious ways. In February, 2014, our team leader ended up not enjoying her new position. YEAH! By the grace of God, a TL had resigned from HSI and the previous team leader was hired for two other sites. This is how good HSI is to staff. They give everyone a second chance.

Between her two sites, enough sleep night hours were available for a full-time position to be considered. She called me and suggested that I should apply internally for the position. She figured I could still work at my current site along with her site until the other night positions opened to continue helping the individual we had been working with for years.

I applied internally for the sleep night position. It was great to be working with her again at a different site. The best part was I knew it would be only a matter of *time* before I would be in a full-time night-position role, and I wouldn't have to be a TL at the old site, WHEW! That was the beginning of more changes to come in the work area of my life.

Gratefully, HSI started the hiring process for all the team leader positions right away. They started with our site first because theyknew

I was going to take the sleep-night hours. The administration didn't want the individual at our site to worry unnecessarily.

Our new team leader for the old site came into the picture early March, 2014. YEAH! I was done with the team leader position. I don't remember ever being so glad **not to** have a position! I was going to do whatever I could to be of service to her.

The first issue our new team leader had to deal with is scheduling the house staff and realizing she needed to do the shopping and appointments. She understood all this and shopped which was a big relief for me. This scheduling plan worked for a while until…

One week later, this was late March, 2014, we had a severe snowstorm coming. Our team leader lived about 30 miles away. I realized she wasn't going to make it in because of the storm, even though she vowed she was going to make it thinking the storm wasn't going to be that bad. C'mon, this is Minnesota!

I knew we needed food. Even though Abbott's limitations after Dr. Traverse's restrictions in February said NO SHOPPING, I thought this one *time* wouldn't hurt. I decided to shop for the whole week because of the storm. I shopped slowly and unloaded the groceries myself.

As I unloaded the groceries, the weather hit. I became extremely exhausted as I unloaded the groceries. I had to fight the weather while I carried in the heavy bags. I unloaded all of the groceries, and put only the food away that needed to be refrigerated. I left the rest of the groceries to put away later when I came back. I wanted to have some *time* off before my next run of long hours began.

I challenged the restriction Abbott gave me of no shopping. I thought shopping the one *time* would be fine. I justified my decision, as I wasn't challenging it to be stubborn, but to help. I learned the next day to pay more attention to doctor's orders; THEY DO KNOW WHAT THEY'RE DOING!

I felt the after-effects of the shopping trip the next day. Although, our new team leader appreciated that the shopping was done, I paid the price. My heartbeat was deliberately slower and stronger.

It continued to beat like that the whole next day. I stayed home and paid close attention to the beat of my heart. I thought I might have to go into the ER or take a nitro tab. I remembered what my heart felt like when I had my heart attack, and I was ready to call 911 again if needed. Gratefully, by the second day, my heartbeat was back to normal.

After that experience of my heart beating so strangely, I told our TL what happened. I told her that NO WAY would I ever do that kind of shopping again. She and I checked into delivery services for shopping. I was okay with smaller loads of shopping, but weekly shopping: NEVER AGAIN!

The strange heartbeat affected me so much that to this day, I won't do shopping. I help put the groceries away, but pushing the cart and dragging the bags in is definitely off limits! Our team leader understood that as she is also an EMT.

I have to add this here even though the story is a different topic. It was a very strong feeling for me, and it happened at work this same *time.* That's why I added the story in this spot. Plus, I wanted to remember it.

Remember how the dietitian at the New Ulm Medical Center had taught me how to stay under the 2,300mg of salt intake a day in cardio rehab. The same day as this shopping trip, after being really good about that low-salt diet business, and because I was feeling better, I decided to cheat on that low-salt intake at work.

I had been so busy with the shopping and weather, I didn't have a chance to pack a low-salt supper. Plus, I didn't want to walk all the way home (2 blocks) to pack one because of the weather. I thought that whatever was on the menu at work wouldn't be so salty.

Pizza was on the menu for supper at the group home. Since Ihadn't had any salt intake all day, I thought it'd be okay to have the pizza.

The salt intake on the back of the pizza box read 700 mg per serving. A serving size was about two-thirds of the pizza. The milligrams were well under the 2300mg intake of my salt restriction, so I tried a piece.

I ate ONE bite of the pizza, and it was HORRIBLE! I thought, "WOW! EW! I can't even figure out how we eat this stuff!" I spit the rest of the pizza out, and threw away the rest of my serving. Even if the salt intake was under my daily allowance, eating that much salt at one *time* taught me a lesson.

After I knew how horrible tasting the pizza was, I felt guilty about giving it to the guys. I knew they were looking forward to it and it was on the menu, so gave it to them anyway. They gobbled it down and loved it! I couldn't believe it!

I've splurged since then with pizza, but I had the same awful reaction due to too much salt. Finally, I gave up on my favorite food altogether! It was truly AWFUL!

After I had accounted for my physical self, and with theremodeling of our house completed, I had another side of the physical area of my life to account for, and that was in the work out area. I realized these bodies are gifts, but I have to take care of mine.

That spring, March 2014, I decided it was time to check into a fitness club membership. Even though I was active during both my positions at work (by walking), I felt I needed to do more, especially with weight lifting.

After I checked most of the local fitness clubs out, I decided to try a fitness center open 24/7. Unfortunately, that meant I had no excuse to miss my 12-times-a-month challenge for the insurance payment, because I could go ANYTIME! DARN!

After being at the fitness club for about a month, I learned even that little bit of a workout made a big difference! I thought at least the physical area of my life was completed for God, but I felt something was still missing.

My answer to that could only happen after more of my physical being was remodeled. What I slowly learned was that even though I needed to remodel all the areas of my life, I could remodel only one area at a *time.*

My physical self needed some work yet. The only way to take care of that area was to participate in the stem cell research project. Only then, could I account for all the areas of my life on a daily basis.

Chapter 29:

Stem Cell Research 2 (B)

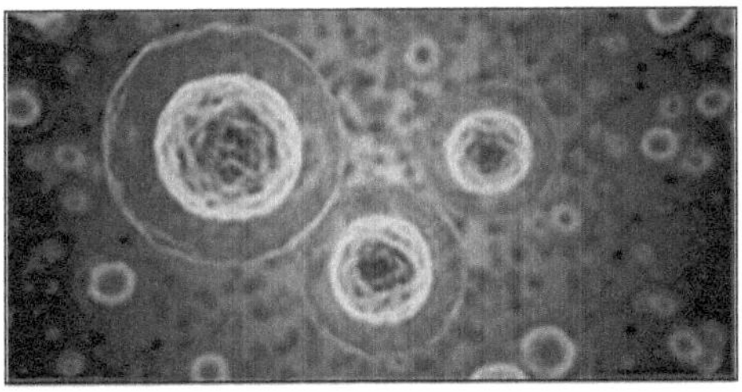

On April 2, 2014, Rose and I drove to the Cities and stayed at my sister's for the night. The next morning, out to Abbott Rose and I go. I check in and they gave me another name bracelet. Rose and I were greeted by Jane. She escorted us into the clinic room. After signing consents, she started the same process with the 25-page report reading and the explanation about that being the randomized Phase of the research study.

Rose was paying more attention to the 25-page report that Jane was reading. I had received another copy at home, and was okay with everything because I participated in the last study. I listened quietly while Jane read.

During that reading, Dr. Henry came, and we greeted each other with hugs. He turned and greeted Rose. Dr. Henry asked, "Do you want to see the program again?"

I agreed, and he led Rose and me into the same room. That *time,* though, it was only us, which was less intimidating than being in a room full of doctors. A few research staff were there, but they didn't say much. It was nice to have fewer people. Rose asked more questions than I.

Dr. Henry gave more of his *time* to show Rose and me how my heart was beating and what he did. I saw red lines that looked like they were going wild. I asked, "What are those red lines for?"

Dr. Henry said, "Those are the stents opening up as I was putting them in."

That was a shorter visit, and it made me feel better. I don't remember what else happened with that visit. Sometimes, when my brain learns too many things at once, it shuts off the rest of the information I want to learn. I watched the program while Rose asked more questions. I enjoyed having Dr. Henry's attention and Jane's attention, by themselves.

After that part of the research, we went back to the exam room, and Dr. Henry listened to my heart. Dr. Henry said, "It sounds great! We'll let you go through the rest of the testing, and see if you qualify by the end of the day."

Off for the MRI and ECHO I went. That *time,* I didn't have the Holter monitor fitting. I was supposed to come back the next day to finish some questionnaires. I would be fitted for the Holter monitor if I qualified.

After the tests, I gave Jane the number of my sister, Paula so she could contact us if any results came in early. We left around 4:30. Rose and I waited at Paula's house.

The weather started to turn nasty: sleeting and snowing. I said a quiet prayer, and thought maybe we could leave for home soon if I happened to be disqualified for the research.

About 2 hours later, a call came from Jane with the results of the study. She said, "Jean, we have good news. Your ECHO changed, but it was for the better. Your ECHO showed your heart pumping from the 40% back in September, 2013 to 54.6% today. And your MRI showed your scar tissue went from 12.6% in September down to 6.6% today. We have to disqualify you again!"

I said, "What? You're kidding!"

She said, "No! We were surprised too, but Dr. Henry and I are so glad for you."

Now, I realized my visit with God was definitely a Near-Death Experience. My experience can't be called anything else. I said, "Wow! We had hoped to leave for home early, and now we can with this snowstorm coming."

Jane said, "Yeah. We've been watching it too."

After I heard those results, I was brave and thought Jane could call the experience I had something. I asked, "Did you read *My Visit with God*?"

Jane said, "Yes. As a matter of fact, I posted it on my bulletin board if you don't mind?"

I said, "Oh, please, do! I don't know what to think." Jane chuckled, "Many people have read that."

I thanked her for believing in me. We said our goodbyes, and I offered her more assistance if needed.

Even though I didn't have a professional term from anyone yet, I had more proof that my visit with God was a Near-Death Experience. Too many "coincidences" happened that morning for it to be considered anything else. My Near-Death Experience was so beautifully designed from Above, and it wa***s absolutely real.***

After I was disqualified for Stem Cell Research twice, I focused more than ever on continuing to fulfill the answer to God's question He gave me when I was with Him: **"What are you going to do for me?"** I had told Him I could still be a better person!

I was positive that accounting for all the areas of my life in a day was how I was going to go to Heaven the next *time* God called me home, because I figured out the answer. I couldn't quite figure out why I had such a hard *time* fulfilling my answer if that was truly the answer.

How on earth was I disqualified for STEM CELL II project? Of course, it is always from GOD. I needed help from my cardio team, plus, the additional physical exercise from my fitness club contributed to the scores improving so much. Yes, I hate to admit that exercise may have saved my life!

Prayers from school children and their staff continued to be said! God and the prayers from everyone led to the quickness of my physical wellness and my being able to have a second chance.

My ECHO changed in November 2013, but instead of my life threatening condition, a procedure implementing 7 stents aided my survival worsened, I continued to improve. The improvement of my health made me appreciate, and want to thank more people again for what they had done for me.

Prayers let me spend more *time* with my family, especially with our grandchildren. Yes, I needed to somehow let everyone know the results. I had only one way to share them.

Chapter 30:

More Thankyous

After being disqualified from Stem Cell Research II, I was even more thankful for prayers. Easter, April, 2014, was coming, and I remembered that the two classes continued to pray for me.

While in Hy-Vee one day, I saw those same candy baskets. I sent one to each of the classes who prayed for me to show my appreciation for their prayers! When I wrote the thank you to the older class, I included the test results of the two studies. Their teacher could explain and compare and contrast the results to them. I thought that might make a good Math lesson!

I heard the teacher had read the results to the class, and that they had big smiles on their faces. I was glad I sent the baskets. I prayed the thank you would have a neat impact on them, and it sounds like it did.

I thought about going up and saying hi to this class one day so they could see I was a real person connected to their prayers that were heard by God. But I haven't met that class and even have been in the school. I never had the nerve to go up and say hi or thank you. I was afraid I would have started to cry. I've always been a behind-the- scenes type of person. By now, I knew if God had wanted me to go to the class, He'd have directed me. Sometimes, things are better left as a mystery.

Two things remained for certain: First, it was nice to learn that THANKYOUS ARE STILL IMPORTANT! I WROTE ONE LITTLE THANK YOU IN THE PAPER, AND THE STORY DEVELOPED INTO A BOOK, BECAUSE THE NEW ULM MEDICAL CENTER'S PUBLIC RELATIONS/MARKETING SPECIALIST KITTY SAW IT, AND USED IT.

Second; MORE IMPORTANTLY, GOD HEARS PRAYERS FROM PEOPLE OF ALL AGES, AND THEY WORK!

I slowly learned to say no to work with HSI, because I needed to spend *time* with my family! In my family life area, I spent more *time* with our grandchildren even in different areas. Our oldest grandchild loved seeing her Grandma Jean teaching preschool at her school right across from her kindergarten room! I also attended her kindergarten graduation Mass! (One of the events I asked God for more *time* to do).

Since the school year ended, I've opened up hours during the day to spend *time* with our grandchildren. I'm hoping subbing will build up when the school year starts.

As my hours shifted to sleep-night positions with HSI, I had more *time* open in the afternoons to help with the grandchildren. Slowly, my *time* with them and my own family will increase. I was frustrated with hours changing, because I wanted to schedule all the areas in my life daily, and for those hours to stay permanent. I wanted the hours to change immediately, because I knew first-hand I was only guaranteed the breath I was taking.

I continued to fulfill the response I gave to God in ALL the areas of my life: family, personal, and most importantly, spiritual!

CHAPTER 31:

CHANGE

MY LIFE CHANGED THE MOST in my spiritual direction! I prayed continuously, and kept my Near-Death Experience foremost in my mind. To everyone else, my SCAD was over. I had no physical scars, my health was fine, and my experience meant nothing. But, to me, my Near-Death Experience was always foremost in my mind.

The SCAD may have been over, but no matter how well I became, the impact from my Near-Death Experience, the prayers, and the medical care were always remembered, and appreciated.

Before I did anything, I prayed that I had done that activity to Glorify God's Name. When I prayed that prayer, it changed my perspective on why I had done things, and how I acted when I was in whatever area of my life I was in, including what the words I said.

I returned as a sacristan once the construction in the church was finished. A few parishioners came up to me, and said they had read my story in the paper or received a copy of *My Visit with God* letter, and were glad to see my return. I was really honored anyone would even notice I was gone.

Parishioners, who saw me most Saturday nights, realized I had been gone for quite some time. They knew something had happened.

I was honored they even knew I had been gone and missed me. They asked how I was doing. That feeling of knowing I had done some good will always be remembered.

My life slowly changed. I was frustrated with that, as, like I said, I already knew my *time* was limited. But whatever I did or said in all areas of my life, I knew was done to fulfill the response I gave to God to be a better person. Yeah. Truly, I had been an idiot. I had taken my life somewhat for granted, and needed God to bring me back to reality and help me remember why I was here.

My problem with figuring out a *time* pattern from the foolproof plan I had was, obviously, that schedules change in a heartbeat. Events that happened were out of my control.

In the spring of 2014, after my STEM CELL RESEARCH II, Easter, and visits from special people, I realized my foolproof plan of still being a better person still needed more *time,* and a clearer view before the answer to God's question, that I could still be a better person, was fully implemented.

But first, other events were about to happen.

CHAPTER 32:

MEDIA/THANKYOUS PART 2

THE SAME WEEK I finished the Stem Cell Research II, on Friday, April 5, 2014, another call came from Kitty, the Marketing/Communications Specialist person at the New Ulm Medical Center.

Kitty said, “Jean, the office of Philanthropy is looking for stories for Allina’s central hospital in the Cities to share with people to help raise money for the hospital. Would it be okay to use your story for this purpose, too? Please call me back and let me know. Thanks.”

I was surprised the marketing department thought my story could do that much good to want to put it in the publication they have in the Twin City hospital for a fundraiser project! I called the next day. She explained what the purpose of the letter would be.

Kitty said, “I know we technically have a year to use your story, because of the consent you already signed but I really wanted you to know why we were using it, and still thought we should have your permission. So, would it be okay to use it again?”

I wanted to continue to show my appreciation for all the New Ulm Medical Center had done for me. I said, “Sure. If it helped, use my story any way you want. I’d like a copy of the letter.”

Kitty laughed and said, "Actually, I think we'll have you come down ,and read it so you know what's going out."

I agreed.

Kitty said she gave my name to another staff person who worked with her in the Foundations department. I received an e-mail the next week. Interestingly, like I knew the LCP at the assisted living facility, the foundation person was someone I knew from working with at the schools. We met the next week and she had a copy of the letter she wanted to use. It was much better as she printed Dr. Rayl's name in it; he deserves a ton of credit.

A copy of my letter was sent to the Philanthropy Department, so they could use it for the Allina hospital publication. A couple weeks later as I was working, one of the residents rang, and I answered her call. When I entered her room, I happened to glance at her stand and there was an Allina mailing on it.

The mailing had my picture on it with the caption JEAN NIELSEN ALLINA PATIENT! I thought, *My, the philanthropy department went all out.* I was taken aback, but didn't say anything to the resident about it being me. It was strange to see my face in that bold of a position which could do that much good.

A couple days later, another copy of my letter came in the mail with a completely different style. They changed the picture, but the form letter was the same. My signature was on the bottom, and they worded it so it came from my words instead of how the Journal wrote it. It made me seem really smart!

Actually, the philanthropy department was pretty creative with the story. The use of different styles made the envelope more eye appealing, so people would want to read the contents, instead of throwing it out! My prayer for this was, I hope it helped!

NEW ULM
MEDICAL CENTER
FOUNDATION

Once again, as I was going to finish writing my story, and put some closure on my Near-Death Experience, but I couldn't. After my story came out for the philanthropy department, more acknowledgments came from the positive side of the media. That made me want to include it in this part of the story. More positive results came during different fests New Ulm celebrated.

CHAPTER 33:

SUMMER 2014

The Bavarian Blast Fest

LIFE ROUTINES WERE SLOWLY returning to normal, until... July 2014. Our annual Bavarian Blast Fest was coming up. That fest was held in July celebrating New Ulm's German culture and the founders of the city.

Rod and I had always helped out with the Knights of Columbus booth. That was quite enjoyable, actually, and a chance to meet a lot of fun people who come from all over. Visitors come from Illinois, Wisconsin, South Dakota, the Cities and yes even bands from Germany come to help celebrate.

The fest as any New Ulm fest, opened with a keg opener sponsored by, of course, our local brewery and with the help of the local battery. The opener was always accompanied by our well-known Concord Singers, sometimes led by our mayor. He was quite the conductor and most of the time his cabinet of singers listened to him!

Over the years, the fest grew and incorporated a parade. That parade became well-known, and lasted more than two hours. It usually had 200 units who came from all over as well.

The best part about the parade was the people! In New Ulm, there's an unwritten law stated that if your house was on the parade route, you hosted families who needed space when hotels and campgrounds were full. Out-of-town people can't believe that type of hospitality.

During New Ulm's Bavarian Blast parade, a couple people saw me and recognized me from the Allina publication. I had thought my notoriety would have faded by then. However, one lady said, "Jean, I see your name and face all over the place lately. It's so good to see you doing so well."

I answered, "Oh, thank you! I'm glad they could use the story to help." Then, she had to run to catch up to her float.

Anyway, when Rod and I signed up to work, we added our names to work with whomever. That particular year, Rod couldn't work and I told our Grand Knight, at the time, who happened to be our bone doctor as we call him, Dr. Mario, if he needed anyone, I'd still help even though technically I wasn't a Knight. He grabbed the opportunity. In New Ulm, people truly didn't care about gender in any club; they all worked together, and that's what made volunteering fun!

At the Knights of Columbus stand, I worked with a gentleman who said he was on the hospital board. Out of all the people I could've been scheduled to work with, I drew a person's name who was on the hospital board. I know that's not a coincidence! After we introduced ourselves to each other he said, "I thought you looked familiar. We heard your story. It really is good to hear.

I told that board member how every cardiologist at Abbott who checked on me those two days I was sedated that had the physicians at the NUMC had not done what they did andprepared me so well, I would not be here.

That led to the other part of the conversation of how I was so tired of hearing all the negativity from stories television and radio aired. He agreed that the negative always outweighs the positive. I agreed and said I wanted the New Ulm Medical Center to know how much good they do too (as with all hospitals)! I was glad my story could help.

It was great fun meeting and working with him. God threw us together to work the same shift. Seriously, I worked with a member of the hospital board! That was the kind of positive exposure to stories the media should use: stories that help people instead of airing the negative side of them all the time.

Almost a year later, because of the media's help, people were commenting on how good it was to hear that our hospital, the New Ulm Medical Center ER department, even as small as it is can still do what they're designed to do: SAVE LIVES and do some good!

Media continued to receive and write positive comments on the good side of my story. Thanks to the media; Even though my story was written primarily for the New Ulm Medical Center, they proved the media could share the good side of the story.

Life continued here, and I hadn't had a chance to talk to our parish priest about my visit with God. I was going to skip it, because too much *time* had gone by, and I figured (like before I had my SCAD, what's the difference, it's no big deal anyway), and I justified my skipping the visit by telling myself, he was busy. Things were calming some. My life continued to be busy, and I thought my spiritual area was completed, so didn't feel the need to talk to him.

However, I had a nagging feeling come over me. I thought that feeling was about hanging up a crucifix on our porch. Interestingly, I hadn't even done that yet. Slowly, I realized there was another side to my Near-Death Experience besides convincing people that it was real.

Still more circumstances came up that put the pieces of the puzzle together, which clarified calling my visit with God a Near-Death Experience! Naming my experience was going to take some assistance, and this assistance was going to come from someone who I thought I didn't need to talk to because I had figured my spiritual area was taken care of.

Chapter 34:

Special Visit

A Visit with our Priest

In July 2014, as I was doing my sacristan duties, a priest who had received a copy of *My Visit with God* was there, and we happened to be visiting about the weather after Mass. Finally, I had the nerve to ask him about some of my experience, and mentioned that I probably should talk to him about all that stuff.

He said, "Yeah, we'll go through it down the road."

He could probably tell I needed more *time* to grasp it all (time that we believe we have until we don't). The other question I had to ask our priest was, "Will you tell me what I went through?" I was cringing here because I still didn't want him to think I was a nut asking that.

My bigger fear was that I had committed a serious sin, because I had no idea what I had gone through, and he was going to send me right to Hell where I would be separated from God forever! Our Catholic faith taught that. I'd have no chance of going to Heaven, once I'd be in Hell. I really wanted a term, so I knew what to expect when I died again.

He said, "What you went through was a Near-Death Experience." Hearing that term Near-Death Experience from him was enough for me. I still haven't really sat down with him about the rest. Frankly,

I needed to write it out first, so it sounded straight, instead of coming

from someone who might think I'm a nut before I visit with him. Who knows! Now, I had a term for what I went through: a Near-Death Experience from clergy.

I thought about asking him what to call the area I was in, but I wasn't sure if I wanted to know. Not yet. I couldn't imagine why God chose me to have one of those Near-Death Experiences. I slowly realized how much my Near-Death Experience was meant for more than trying to convince anyone that God and Heaven exist, but people already believed! I began to realize how much it was meant for me!

I had to come to terms with why I forgot I was here. That was going to take some work, though, and a couple more visits were under way with people who had had a major impact in my recovery.

As I learned, more events were being arranged. The New Ulm Medical Center's Marketing/Communications Specialist person and her partner were working on a special assignment for me, which I didn't know about until later.

Chapter 35:

Intermission

August 26, 2014

Exactly one year since that fateful day, I had hoped to be done writing this. Interestingly, people had forgotten it was my anniversary day. My oldest sister called. Others may have remembered, but maybe they didn't know how or if they should respond. As of 7:00 pm, my husband and children had not said anything, but I guessed they felt it. I think they knew, but who knows?

That day was also Lola's first day of first grade. I made sure to go, because I missed her first day last year! I was at my daughter's plenty early, because I wanted to be there for Lola's special day. I hadn't wanted to disappoint her again.

Once we arrived at school, we had to take pictures. I had great fun seeing old and new faces. We snapped a lot of pictures of Lola at her desk. Her teacher was the same one she had for preschool, so Lola was pretty excited to have her.

Lola met old friends and the day was beautiful. I was so glad to be there. It definitely brought back memories. Emily, our baby granddaughter, came with, of course. She was in on the picture business. I had asked for the day off work to be sure it didn't interfere with being at school.

The first day of school was full of excitement, and we reconnected with teachers. A couple of teachers smiled and hugged me. I'm sure they remembered the event, but they talked about our grandchild, which was great. That was better than dealing with the worry of what happened.

How did I feel? I actually felt heavy. I found it hard to believe that at that point and time— exactly a year ago— I was with God. I was out, unaware of my surroundings or earthly being. I felt strange, as I realized all I had been through, particularly as I recognized that I was made of two parts: spiritual and physical.

Mom called, too. My visit with Mom and Dad was so nice. It was nice to be remembered. I realized I'm important to someone.

I opened an e-mail from a dear friend. She sent an article titled, "If Tomorrow Starts without Me". Interestingly, she had sent it a while back, but, for whatever reason, I waited to open it until my first anniversary of my Near-Death Experience. Wow, the title alone surely hit home.

The story reminded me how I should treat people every time I see them. Instead of believing I had as much *time* as I wanted with friends and family, I realized I should treat them with the kindness and goodness they deserved; because those words could be the last words I ever said to them.

After being at Lola's first day of school, I realized everyone else would go on with their lives with or without me, and they should. I would go on with my life, too. I was amazed that a year had passed. I had wanted more significant changes in all areas of my life for each 24-hour period. My life was slowly changing. Organizing my life required *time*: family, friends, work, and new/other employment opportunities, especially with working with children.

August 27, 2014 was a day I hadn't seen last year. I found it strange to think that I had no idea what was going on with my family and friends. Wow, I often wondered what it must be like for someone who was sedated for a longer period of *time*.

August 27, 2013 was and remains difficult. A whole day gone with no memory of it: a blank space in my mind. I tried focusing on living for today. Now, I truly hope I had done some good.

Living the answer to God's question for me remained my goal. My life will be lived to fulfill the response I gave to God as to how I could still be a better person IN ALL AREAS OF MY LIFE DAILY!

I thought I understood what I needed to do here, before my SCAD, and how to live all the areas of my life. Now, I focused on reevaluating why I decided to do what I'm doing. First, though, I needed more closure before I could do that. Closure was going to come with another visit from a special person.

CHAPTER 36:

A VISIT WITH DR. RAYL

WOW! THE MARKETING AND COMMUNICATIONS SPECIALIST person from the New Ulm Medical Center e-mailed me on Wednesday, September 3, 2014, with the possibility of some dates I could actually meet with Dr. Rayl. I wasn't sure what I was going to say, but I wanted to find out what he did, and what happened that would make every cardiologist at Abbott, a major heart hospital, say, "Had New Ulm not done what they did or lagged one step, you wouldn't be here!" Maybe meeting Dr. Rayl would bring some closure for me.

Primarily, I wanted to thank Dr. Rayl again. I know I thanked him with the Easter baskets and cookies, but the anticipation of meeting someone who saved my life was overwhelming. People never seem to receive enough credit for what they do.

My sister e-mailed me pictures of when I was dead in the hospital. I had never seen anyone medically sedated like that before, and boy I was out: dead. When I saw myself sedated like that, I thought, *Whew! The breathing tube etc. was scary. I didn't know anything that was going on around me or to me. My family saw to it that I was in good hands.*

The doctors and nurses cared for me, people prayed, and I came back to life. That made me think and appreciate what the power of prayer had done. I was and am blessed, and I learned to appreciate, every minute, but also every second of the day. **I WAS ONLY GUARANTEED EACH BREATH I HAD TAKEN! After all, I was living on *time* I had borrowed from God.**

I thought I had appreciated everything everyone had done, but when I was so affected by pictures of my death, a new appreciation of life crept into my perspective. I decided to thank my sister in an extra special way one day for her giving me those pictures.

I understood now why Louise said they were horrible pictures and why she didn't want to share them with me! My family stood by and looked at me like that for two days. Those pictures reminded me, though, of what could happen in a heartbeat. Maybe they could help people realize how precious life is.

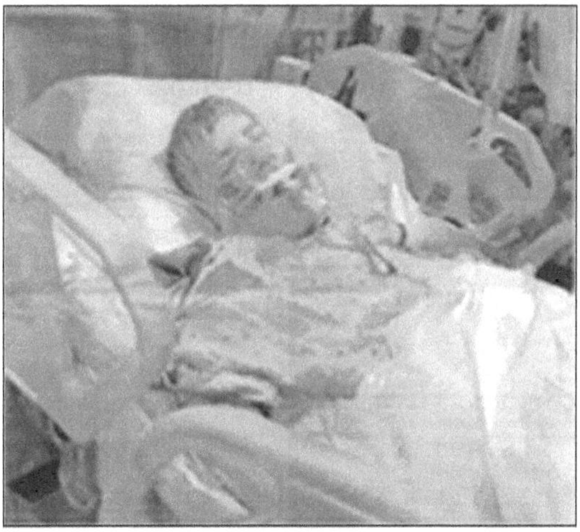

I finally met Dr. Rayl. He gave a hug and told me about more of our visit. Dr. Rayl said, "When you came, you were drenched in sweat: big time— drenched in sweat."

I said, "Really? I just started sweating out at the assisted living facility."

Apparently, from the onset of the attack— from 12:25-12:30 a.m. to 1:30 a.m.— my body changed that fast. I was drenched in sweat. I didn't remember most of the ER visit. I looked at him and said, "Oh. Was that why you told everyone I looked like Hell."

He smiled.

I said, "And you shocked me twice in the ER room." That was from information in the ER report.

Dr. Rayl mentioned my family didn't remember what happened, because they were in the lounge area most of the time. He told me more that happened in the emergency room. Dr. Rayl's explanation definitely confirmed the *dying* comment in his part of the article. I needed that information from his visit to justify my experience being called a Near-Death Experience.

Then Dr. Rayl asked me what I remembered. I told him my story. Dr. Rayl said, "Yeah. You were in and out of it. You also complained of being nauseated— big time, too."

I said, "I don't remember that."

He shook his head yes to confirm I had mentioned that I was nauseated. Then Dr. Rayl said, "I'm so glad everything turned out as it did."

The foundation chair came in and wanted our picture. We had our pictures taken.

I thanked him again and gave him one of my candy baskets that he could share with the staff.

Dr. Rayl left then. He had to go to his next shift. I very much appreciated the information he shared and that he had taken the *time* to meet with me. That was typical of the patient care at the New Ulm Medical Center: doctors taking *time* to meet individually with patients.

I visited with our foundation chair, and thanked her for her *time* too. I felt strange after that visit, but I was glad to know the rest of my story.

I had some closure after meeting Dr. Rayl, and having a visit with our priest. Once again, I was going to finish writing this story then, but never had the chance.

Still, something was nagging at me, but I had no idea what I still missing. I thought all my 24-hour life changes were complete. Little did I know that my Near-Death Experience and second chance at life meant more than I had first believed.

Chapter 37:

January 2015 Experiences

Another/Second Chance

After the Holidays for 2014, I seemed to be established in a daily routine. But, there was a reason my story wasn't finished: that became much clearer during the winter of 2015.

January 2015 rolled around. That year was a different and difficult kind of winter. The winter was colder, rainier, and icier rather than snowy. That kind of weather could cause as much agony or more as having a lot of snow.

One morning, Rod called. His call was unusual because he was working. He said he was in the emergency room at the New Ulm Medical Center. I panicked. Rod said, "Don't worry. I only broke my ankle."

I asked, "How? Do you want me to come? Does someone from work have to be there? What do you want me to do?"

Rod said, "You can come to the emergency room. I fell walking outside with another client. I got a ride from another supervisor who happened to drive by when I fell, and that's how I got to the hospital."

The Emergency Room at the New Ulm Medical Center was fairly small where Rod was. Rod was calm; actually, the whole ER staff was calm. I honestly didn't know how they could stay so calm in those situations, but they did. Rod had broken his ankle. He had surgery the next day, which went fine. He received six pins and two screws or something like that. A couple days later, he was able to go home.

The day he came home, I had to find a way to walk Rod inside our house. Of course, the difference between finding a way into the house between his incident, and mine, safely, was that now it had snowed. Murphy's Law in effect for me.

One chore I was supposed to avoid with my restrictions from Abbott was shoveling. Well, it was a light snow, and I didn't want to bother any of the neighbors to do that, so I tried myself. I shoveled about half the sidewalk and discovered that was all I could do. I told him how much I had shoveled.

Rod said, "That's fine. It can't be that bad."

Well, "it" (the weather) wasn't the only issue we had. We learned quickly how much work a broken ankle was, especially when the patient is in his late 50s. WOW!

With the help of our neighbor, we walked him into the house safely. Then we settled him in the same place I was only a few short months earlier: in the basement. After Rod was settled, I ran some errands. He was going to have a cast and crutches for six weeks, of course.

I couldn't have guessed how much extra work that broken ankle was for me. I was glad to do it, mind you. Rod was my husband, and, if I could do it for anybody, I would. After all, that's what couples do for each other: they help!

Rod's broken ankle was only over a year from when I had my SCAD. My second chance at HSI of working sleep nights had been scheduled. I was trained in at the site. I had a full schedule. I was working 8-16 hours overtime each week, because the house was so short-staffed.

That was a lot of *time*, but the new team leader there scheduled me mostly for sleep nights: that's what I could do. That was a blessing, because now I had to do extra work around our house, too.

All our neighbors pitched in as they could with the shoveling. MRCI department heads found a job for Rod, because this could possibly be a worker's comp issue. Rod could go to work and at least answer phones.

He loved going to work but secretly, I prayed they wouldn't find any work for him. I was selfish, but I didn't want the extra effort of driving him to work when I was working extra hours at the group home.

I stayed awake after a 10pm-6am to take Rod to work then pick him up at 3:00 p.m. This schedule worked the best, as I didn't have to be back to work until 4:00 p.m. After a couple days of that, Rod realized how exhausted I was. I couldn't keep up that pace along with all the routine household chores.

Rod asked his coworkers to help drop him off or pick him up from work. Having their help transporting Rod helped a great deal. I felt guilty needing all this help again, but what could I do?

Rod had difficulty sleeping in the basement, so tried convincing me into letting him sleep upstairs. The only way to accomplish Rod's climbing the stairs to the bedroom safely was by crawling. He tried going down the stairs once using the crutches and fell. That fall scared me.

I realized we needed to think about downsizing fast. Our beautiful newly-remodeled home wasn't going to be ours for life. We had finished remodeling it to the way we wanted the house to be as long as we lived. Now, I was seriously considering selling it! What? That wasn't in my plan.

Selling our house was difficult to think about, but staying in it started to scare me, especially after Rod fell. It wasn't safe to think of staying there through old age, especially when I thought of going through normal aging issues: knee replacements, hip replacements, etc. Rod's broken ankle forced us to face making long-term life decisions whether we were ready or not.

Thankfully, a friend caught us at Mass one night and happened to think of us. He knew of my SCAD and Rod's dilemma, and asked if we had thought about selling. He knew the design of our house, and what we truly wanted. He had a house for sale with everything on the main floor, for which we were looking.

Jim also mentioned the location. It was two blocks from Louise's and Bruce's. We went to look at it that Friday. I realized that selling our house might be an actual possibility, so I went to the bank to start the paper work for pre-approval for a loan.

Our ages, accesses, credit scores, and accounts that we had with the bank made the pre-approval process fast and easy. Now, all we needed was to find a new house and sell ours?

The house Jim showed was perfect for me but too much house. Even though the money was okay with the pre-approved amount the bank would loan us, it was steep. I didn't care about any of that and was ready to buy anything just to get out of our current house: FAST!

Our previous experience of buying houses, especially a rambler in New Ulm, was difficult at best. Buying a rambler quickly— even if the loan was steep— showed how much our house scared me. As long as another house had all we needed on the main floor, and was technically in our price range, I was done with our current house. Our present house was definitely built for a younger couple. Even though the new house wasn't quite right (it was too big, and the price was steeper than we wanted), the showing started the ball rolling.

Looking for new housing created some tension between Rod and me. He was reluctant to make an offer on anything, whether it had all the space we wanted on the main floor or not. Finally, Rod admitted that he was stalling on selling the house because he wanted to stay in the neighborhood.

Of course, I wanted to stay in the neighborhood, as well, but I could not see us staying where we were. It was too dangerous! At one point, I almost gave up on the idea of moving, because Rod was so unwilling to leave the neighborhood, until…

God had other plans! One Saturday evening, I was going out the other end of the alley, which I never do, it *so happened* that I had parked my car in that direction, and thought it was easier to go straight instead of turning around. When I drove to the end of the alley, I looked both ways. As I looked to the left, I saw that rambler on our block was for sale. I couldn't believe it! The *For Sale* sign had gone up as I looked at it.

I was surprised that the rambler had gone up for sale, because the couple who bought it only bought it about a year ago. They were excited to be on the block. I contacted our Realtor, immediately, to see if I may had been mistaken about that rambler. He emailed me back the same night, and said he would find out specifics.

He emailed back with all the specifics. The house had all the space we needed, sat on a one-half lot, which meant less lawn/shoveling, and the price was lower than what we would receive for selling our house!

The family scheduled an open house on Tuesday. I emailed him back, and said we'd meet him there at 5:00p.m. Finally, I had the nerve to talk to Rod about it again. He hadn't seen it, and was still reluctant. I said, "I saw the house at the end of the block for sale. There's an open house Tuesday, and I'm going to go look at it." Do you want to come? It's only an open house. If you don't like it, we don't have to buy it, but it's on the same block. We would be foolish not to at least look at it."

That house was a Godsend. It solved both of our dilemmas: Rod wanting to stay on the block, and mine wanting all the space on the main floor.

At 5:00 p.m., we walked to the house, and 4 other couples were behind us. It was perfect. We put a proposal on the house that night without contingencies. The next day, the family accepted our offer. By the end of the week, the house was ours. Even though I know everything comes from God. That house going up for sale on the same block was an absolute, Godsend!

We put our house up for sale, and it sold in four weeks, because we had the whole house redone! Boy, was I ever glad Rod and I decidedto remodel the house! We moved around the corner on the same block: literally around the corner. We had a couple of remodeling projects for the new house, but they went quickly. (I'll never say we'll never have another remodeling project, again)!

In March, 2015, in the process of remodeling, our current house, my schedule started opening up. I dropped my current positions with both assisted living places, since they both were full staffed. The girls were on their way with their own schedules, and didn't need my help anymore.

One day, while exercising, I met a couple of ladies through the maintenance man from work. They all belonged to the Lion's Club, and started talking about their upcoming membership drive.

After they asked me if I wanted to join the Lions, I wondered about the gender issue. Gary said the members' wives would help with fundraisers etc., so the men in New Ulm decided to let them join. I agreed to check it out. The Lions Club impressed me right away. I knew quite a few of them from around the community and church, so I felt comfortable being there.

I checked with my team leader at HSI to see if I could be assured of having the second Thursday off every month. She said I could. Joining the Lion's Club was another second chance. I had belonged to clubs up north before and enjoyed it. I could join, because of having my evenings opened. I involved myself right away helping with projects to find a CURE for diabetes, hearing and vision and other developmental delays. The Lion's Club members are a very proud group; many have been there for over 20 years!

One night in March, 2015, before we started the process of our move, I was enjoying our newly modeled basement when a phone call from a friend brought the reality as to why we should treat each other as miracles!

She started talking like it was going to be a normal visit, just to chat. She had an ominous tone in her voice. She finally told me that the son of a close friend of ours had died in a horrible car accident. We cried together for a long time.

A few days later, I called and talked to them for quite a while. It was horrible to hear the tears and grief they were going through again. They had lost their home in a fire. I felt helpless. Since they lived up north, Rod and I couldn't go to them, because the weather was too risky. We had no way to help them.

The one thing I could do, even if all hope seemed lost, was pray for them, and I asked others to do the same. Prayer was the one thing I could always do, because I believed and knew first-hand that prayer works. After all, I'm living proof!

A couple months later, Rod and I drove up for a visit. Because it was Memorial Day weekend, we were going up to take care of Rod's folks' grave. That gave us a chance to visit our suffering friends, too.

We decided to pick up supper before we went there, so they wouldn't have to worry about feeding everyone. They had all their grandchildren there. Although our friends were still grieving, their grandchildren and extra company helped lighten the atmosphere and gave us something else on which to focus. They shared their experiences, then, instead of being focused on their loss, they asked how my health was. I said I was fine.

At one point, I talked to her husband and said something to make him laugh. I can't remember what that was, but he and I laughed for the longest time. I think we ended the night around midnight. It was good to hear them laugh.

My friend showed us lots of pictures of the event they had taken and received. I wondered why I had a second chance when a life so young didn't? A stark reminder to me as to how precious life is every moment!

Back home, more changes at HSI started to occur. Even though, I had switched most of my hours to the other site, I continued working one morning every two weeks at my old site. That was because the team leader needed me, and the client did, too. And I needed him.

When that same client was taken to the hospital a few weeks later, I went to see him. He looked well. He knew me, and we visited. His health situation deteriorated fast, though, and led to placing him in hospice at his home.

I had been this client's mainstay staff for 14 years! My taking care of him during his hospice days would have been too emotional for me, especially after my own Near-Death Experience, and the recent loss of my friend's son. Thankfully, other agencies and people stepped in to help him.

After my Near-Death Experience, words and actions weren't mere words and actions anymore. Everything brought on a new heightened awareness. Life meant more. My words and actions meant more in what I said and did with people in ALL areas of my life.

Why was I still writing this? I thought I had the answer to being a better person when I tried to schedule all the areas of my life in a 24-hour day. The complete answer I sought to give God was going to come from still more signs. Those signs showed me more fully what I should be doing in all the areas of my life, and why I needed this second chance!

CHAPTER 38:

ALL IN ALL

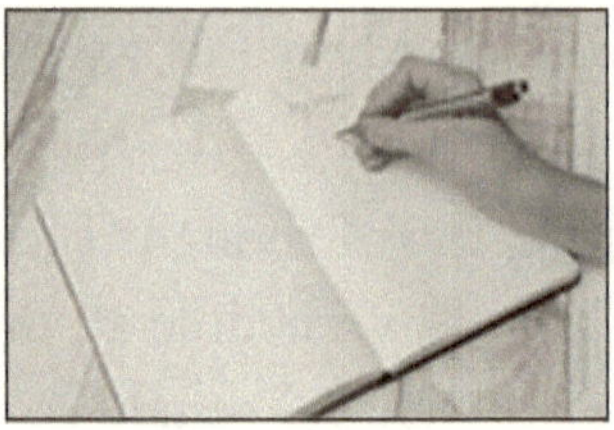

CONTINUOUSLY AND CONSTANTLY, my hours shifted in all the areas of my life. What I thought was a good schedule changed; and the *time* I wanted to spend with everyone became limited and even non-existent due to my work responsibilities and others' schedules.

I felt discouraged, frustrated, inadequate, and challenged because I couldn't account for all the areas of my life in every 24-hour day. I had my back against the wall as I faced my impossible challenge. I had not felt like this before my SCAD, but I had a sense of urgency to figure out a foolproof schedule, immediately, and make my schedule permanent.

I thought I had the answer in the lyrics to the song, "Shout to the Lord". I could not understand why I continued to fail in accounting for all the areas of my life in a 24-hour day until God gave me more signs.

Lyrics to another song started going through my mind that spring, reminding me that God was my strength. One day, I asked God ifthat song was meant for me to give me another sign (I'm big into signs). Rod and I were off to Mass. Before Mass, the accompanist sometimes plays music to set the mood. Of course, the first song she played was the very song I heard in my head.

I thought hearing that song at Mass was a fluke. Sure enough, she kept playing the song over and over. I thought, *I have to quit asking for signs!* I knew the song was meant for me, though. The worst part was, now I needed to figure out what the words in the song meant.

I had a difficult *time* as I tried to figure out the meaning to that song. Then, God gave me another sign (probably because I had such a difficult *time* figuring out meanings in songs). Instead of the next sign being in a song, I noticed a particular number that resurfaced over and over: 3.

For instance, I experienced three drops from the helicopter on my way to Minneapolis.

God's voice came from clouds that were in a V-formation— a triangle— three sides.

The silhouettes of the voices that came through were outlined in groups of three.

Three appeared even in the year of my dissection: 2013. The nurse at Abbott gave me three Senna tabs.

I heard a helicopter land three times when I was on the fifth floor. My favorite NFL football team, the Green Bay Packer's morals and values came in very specific order as three: God, family, then the

Green Bay Packers. *(*Listed in books written by players*)*

At the time I wrote this, it had been over three years since my SCAD.

It's amazing, that as we're finding out more about SCAD, there are 3 SCAD survivors at that *time* of mine, who survived, and came from the New Ulm Medical Center. A medical center considered relatively small. The three of us were able to meet for lunch.

Abbott only sees 3-5 SCAD patients per year— and 2-3 don't live!

Our oldest grandchild was in third grade and the second one was three!

I remembered asking God for more *time* in case we would have any other grandchildren. Our third grandchild was here— a GIRL— and she was five-weeks-old!

Most importantly, we have a Tri-une God: Father, Son, and Holy Spirit.

The list goes on. Three was significant. I thought there must be a reason for that number to keep coming up.

That's why I couldn't go to Heaven yet. I had to finish on Earth what I was supposed to do: not my will, but God's Will. I finally learned that it was okay if I didn't have all the areas of my life included in one 24-hour day. The meaning had to do with *how* I was living all the areas of my life.

I needed to realize how my sin affected more people than myself, my sin affected everyone! I needed to go back to Confession, and admit I chose to commit that sin of skipping it while serving the congregation as a Eucharistic Minister, sacristan and a parishioner (three roles, by the way, of the Catholic Church). Living in God's grace means more than picking and choosing the sacraments in which I wanted to participate; I needed to practice ALL of them, because, my sins affected three types of people: me, you, and more importantly, God! That's why the number 3 was so significant!

I was amazed that I needed so many people working and praying together to help me remember why I was here. No wonder God needed to give me more signs; to help me find the true meaning to my response. God needed to show me through the words in the songs I heard while in the hospital how I needed to live All the areas of my life for God.

CHAPTER 39:

GREATNESS/MIRACLES

I HADN'T THOUGHT of my being any kind of miracle. I'm a firm believer in miracles, but I figured my family was kidding about that anyway. People say lots of things when someone is in a tragic situation, and I figured telling me I was a M-I-R-A-C-L-E were only words.

After I survived my SCAD, everyone was telling me what a miracle I was and that God had something great for me to do.

Doctors at Abbott were telling my family what a miracle I was. Dr. Henry told me what I had done for New Ulm was great.

Our priest told me he heard I was a miracle.

The pharmacist at the New Ulm Medical Center was telling me how great I was.

The dietitian at the New Ulm Medical Center was telling me I was going to do something great yet.

Dad told me I was going to do something great!

After hearing about all of this greatness, and more importantly having a Near-Death Experience and writing *My Visit with God*, one would think I would be elated! All my jobs were finished. I wrote the thank you for the paper and New Ulm Medical Center, and best of all, I found the true meaning for the reason I was on Earth.

Suddenly, I remembered *how* to live my spiritual area fully and that area could be lived only with more help. That help came from PRAYER. When people worked together, much goodness could be accomplished. I realized that no matter what life brought, my taking out all the goodness of a tough situation would remind me where I was, how I was supposed to live, and why I existed.

The greatness and miracle everyone was talking about really wasn't anything I had done by conquering death or having a Near-Death Experience, but the greatness each person can have when working with others to help one another to Heaven. The greatness for me was I realized I needed to live all the areas of my life as God Wills, not mine.

The final answer to the question God had for me when I was with Him, **"What are you going to do for me?"** was truly to still be a better person. The only way I could do that was— instead of believing I needed to schedule all the areas of my life in 24-hour each day— was to practice ALL the sacraments the Church gave us as the Catholic church teaches in "Full Communion of the Church", because that was how I was to live my life- fully in God's grace.

But I will need help again because of sins I may commit. The true greatness for me will be knowing with people's help, I'll go to Heaven. The joy in heaven will be everlasting.

While the greatness for me will be home in Heaven, by living All. The areas of my life in "full Communion of the Church," that can only be done because God gave His greatest gift: Jesus!

Chapter 40:

The Way of the Cross

THIS INFORMATION is taken from a brochure distributed from the Diocese of New Ulm by the Knights of Columbus.

The Way of the Cross is a shrine of the Catholic Diocese of New Ulm. It is a shrine leading up a gentle incline of Loretto Hill, adjacent to the New Ulm Medical Center. This is the site of the Way of the Cross.

The shrine was built in 1904, and retells the story of Christ's trial, crucifixion, and death in life-like images portrayed in statuary. The fourteen stations, grotto, and Lady of Sorrows Chapel were created by the Sisters of the Order of the Poor Handmaids of Jesus Christ, who owned and managed Loretto Hospital and St. Alexander Home for the aged. The Loretto Hospital has become the present New Ulm Medical Center. The home for the aged has been razed from the site. What remains is the Way of the Cross Shrine. The shrine is now owned by the Diocese of New Ulm.

Each station consists of a brick structure with a small peaked roof topped by a Celtic cross. Cement pillars on each side support a rustic arch completing an enclosure for the statuary tableau, representing various scenes in the Passion of Christ. A nameplate below bears the title of the scene.

The project was initiated by Father Alexander Berghold and sister Flavia of the Poor Handmaids. A great deal of credit must go to Sister Flavia's untiring efforts of leadership in accomplishing the building of the shrine. Construction began in 1903 and was completed in 1904. The Sisters were responsible for excavating and preparing much of the construction site. They pushed wheelbarrows up the hill, transporting cobblestones used in the construction of the stations, pathway, and rock walls.

Ideally located midway up the Loretto Hill is the grotto in honor of Our Lady of Lourdes as she appeared to Saint Bernadette. At the summit is the chapel dedicated to the Sorrowful Mother. At this point, tourists may enjoy a beautiful view of the city of New Ulm and the Minnesota River Valley.

The object of the Stations of the Cross, which dates back to the Middle Ages, is to help Christians make, in spirit, a pilgrimage to the scenes of Christ's suffering and death in Jerusalem. Devout individuals may be seen passing from Station to Station, kneeling at each to meditate on the scene.

The Way of the Cross is a picturesque pathway through a wooded hillside leading to a small brick and stone chapter. The above information was taken from a brochure published by the Diocese of New Ulm.

We all have many crosses to bear. I realized my cross was, and continues to be, even though I had gone back to Confession to be reconciled to you and God, how skipping Confession affected all of you serving the Church as a sacristan, Extraordinary Eucharistic Minister of Communion, and as a parishioner.

You expected me to be in "Full Communion of the Church", while serving in all those roles- (the number three again comes up here), and I wasn't. I chose to participate in the Sacraments I wanted. God knew I would commit sins, and that's why He had to send a very special gift.

God sent His son, Jesus to save us from all our sins. Jesus will always remember his people. We may not have a peaceful world all the *time,* because of sin. But everyone worked together for my sake, which brought me closer to God and Heaven. That, to me, would be greater than anything I could do on Earth.

I am only one person, just an average Catholic-born-Wisconsin-native-German-Irish-Swiss-Luxembourger-Green Bay Packer fan, but by living in God's grace by receiving all of God's Sacraments— not the ones I choose— through my service to my church, my community, and my family, I can make where we live here in New Ulm, Minnesota, a more loving and peaceful place through love, laughter, and prayers. There's only one place I would want to live to continue to still be a better person, and change my sinfulness because

TO MY FAMILY AND ME LIVING IN NEW ULM, MINNESOTA, IS LIKE— AS THE TITLE OF THE BOOK STATES—

ALMOST TO HEAVEN!

God bless us all!

AMEN.

More Prayer List/Stories

In the following part, I am uncertain as to the order this happened and who contacted whom! I've asked family to share their stories with me regarding this point but life continued. A couple of family did, though, Mom, Dad, and Paula.

Generally speaking, this is what happens when anything goes on in our family. All those people received a thank you and copy of *My Visit with God* dated and signed. That was the start of *My Visit with God* being shared. For this section, in the back of the book, stories are here for all to enjoy!

As mentioned, Louise called our church's phone number and added me on the coordinator's prayer list. Then, Louise called my team leader at the group home. She told her what was going on so she could find someone to replace my shifts.

Then Louise called Rose, our youngest, to tell her to go to Abbott. Once Rose received this call, she tried to contact my other sisters in the Cities. Rose called my sister, Paula, who at first didn't answer. After all, it was around 4:00 am and who calls anyone at this hour. Since Paula didn't answer, Rose called Paula's husband Dave because Dave always answers his phone: Whew, thanks, Dave!

Rose told Dave what happened and that she wanted Paula to come to Abbott since she wanted someone there at the hospital. He woke Paula and said, "Get up! Jean's had a heart attack, and you have to go to Abbott NOW!"

Paula said, "Jean who?" She never expected me to be a heart attack patient. I was a 52- year-old healthy female. **I was 5'2 at 115 lbs. I did not smoke and had normal cholesterol levels, BP, etc.**

Dave said, "Your sister, Jean." Paula said, "Jean, sweet Jean?" She was finally getting her bearings, and she and Dave dressed feverishly. They arrived and started calling the rest of my family. While at the hospital, Paula called Mom and Dad first, of course.

Mom and Dad immediately put me on prayer chains in Bemidji, Minnesota. Mom called her church prayer-chain committee and also the ladies in her bridge club to put me on their prayer lists. Then, Mom and Dad drove to Abbott. Two groups of people praying for me, St. Philip's prayer group and mom's bridge group.

Paula called my sister, Barb, who is the principal of Nativity of Mary in Bloomington. She's the next closest to Abbott. Barb arrived right away too. She called her school and had their teachers and staff start prayer for me. Barb stayed at Abbott for most of that morning and arrived even before Rod. Now, I realized more prayers are being said for me and from a whole school.

Barb has two children Laura and David. Laura is already at college in the state of Wisconsin but David was home. David came to visit me on Tuesday that week as he told me in a later letter. Those two prayed for me as well. Thanks, Barb, Laura, and David!

Paula called our oldest sister, Nancy who was in a meeting at the time. Her client "happened" to be an ER doctor and had been one for over 30 years. Yep, Nancy just "happened" to be with an ER doctor. When Nancy received the call, her assistant, immediately packed her paperwork right away and made transportation arrangements.

Nancy called people from here. Nancy called the Shrine's coordinator in LaCrosse to have them put me on their prayer list. This shrine was managed by an order of nuns who have a sister city in Africa. This sister city also said prayers for people in need! This act of adding me to the sister city prayer list made me realize that people in another state, Wisconsin but another country prayed for me, Africa prayed for me. The list continues.

Nancy also called one of her friends in La Crosse with whom she walked. Her friend belonged to the Jewish synagogue in La Crosse. Nancy told her what happened with me and asked her if her synagogue had a prayer group or something. Her friend said, "Sure!" and added me to the list. Now, one more person and another religion prayed for me Jewish. This act from Nancy's friend made me realize how another faith was involved and prayed for me and they didn't even know me or cared what my religion was!

Nancy then called her husband, Shawn in LaCrosse. Shawn started praying in LaCrosse, Wisconsin. He contacted his daughter, whose name happens to be Rose, too. She lived in Chicago, Illinois. Yes, if you think it is tough being a Packer fan in New Ulm, imagine what it's like being a Packer fan in Chicago, Bear territory!

One night after I was home, Nancy called and said, "Do you know how many people prayed for you?"

I said, "Oh, I don't know, a few?"

Nancy said, "You had hundreds of people praying for you?"

I thought *"Ha. Me! Why? I hadn't done anything great. I'm only a Wisconsin-native, Catholic-born, German, Irish, Swiss, Luxembourgian, Green Bay Packer fan. Why would all those people pray for me?"*

Shawn continued contacting people too. He called his mom, Rosemary, in LaCrosse, to let her know what's going on with me. Now two more people are praying for me and in one more state, Illinois.

Meanwhile, at Abbott, Paula contacted our sister, Jill, in Arizona. Jill contacted her husband, Clark who "happened" to be in the cities on business.

Later, I found out Clark had a mission to talk to the head nurse and make sure I had all the right and top of the line equipment. He worked for a medical supply company so knows all the best equipment out there. The nurse assured him I had the best of all their equipment, and then he felt okay to go. Thanks, Clark!

My sister, Jill is now contacted their three children. Julia is in Washington, Scott in Texas, and Sarah in Alabama. Three more people prayed for me and in three different states, Alabama, Washington and Texas.

Paula contacted her three children too. Lauren is home from college in Iowa. Jack, my godson, is in college in Missouri and Grant was a senior in high school in Edina. Paula sent pictures to them with her phone with Rod's permission so they realized the significance of my illness and started praying for me. Now, three more people prayed for me, and another state involved, Missouri!

By now, Rod was at the hospital and called his immediate family too. He has a brother, Randy, and his wife, Clare, in Boston, a sister, Dawn and husband, Mike, in Connecticut, and a sister and husband and two sons with families in Colorado, Deanna and Larry. Among Rod's immediate family, and his nieces and nephews, twelve more people prayed for me, and three more states included; Colorado, Connecticut, and Massachusetts.

Clare told me later that she called her mom as she belonged to a church's prayer group. She asked her mom to put me on that list. She said in a later conversation, "When you sent your Christmas letter out, I sent the information to mom to share with the group so they could learn what was going on." Now, another group of people prayed for me in three more states, Massachusetts, Connecticut, and Colorado and another faith, too!

Between Nancy and Mom, they called aunts, uncles, and cousins on mom's side of the family. This is no easy feat! Mom has ten brothers and sisters, and out of the ten, one is a nun and two have died. Among all my family on Mom's side, over 80 people who prayed for me. An additional state of California was added to my prayer list.

When my aunt, who is a nun out in California, received her call from Nancy who asked her to add me to her order's prayer chain, she said, "Absolutely" and added me to the Sisters of the Holy Names of Jesus and Mary an order to which there are over 200 nuns.

On my Dad's side, the Murphy side, among all of my aunts, uncles, cousins, and their children, there are over 25 people who prayed for me and this family added me to other prayer lists. An additional state of Virginia was included of people who prayed for me!

Rod called his aunts and uncles, cousins on his mom's side. Amongst all of this family, over 50 more people who prayed for me. They live in the states of Minnesota, North and South Dakota. More and more prayers from family and two additional states were involved. All of those people knew me and couldn't understand why I had a heart attack!

CO-WORKERS WHO PRAYED

Meanwhile, the (LCP) lead care manager at the assisted living facility contacted our team lead to let her know I left via ambulance this morning and might not be at work. The LCP was also concerned as she hadn't heard anything about my status. Remember, this was a new position for me and I think Rod and Louise forgot to call them. The LCP worked for Habilitative Services for 13 years so I knew her from HSI. I was so grateful she was LCP, at the assisted living facility. I had known from working with her at HSI she wouldn't think I was a nut when I called in sick on my first shift off training.

The HSI team leader informed the assisted living facility LCP that I was airlifted to Abbott and had emergency surgery. By now, they knew I had 7 stents and was out of surgery but listed as critical. I might not make it. The LCP couldn't understand how I had been through all this. Granted, in a later conversation with the LCP she said, "I looked pretty tough when the EMTs came." She knew I was in good physical condition and just wasn't expecting anything like this. She informed the rest of the staff out at the assisted living facility about my condition and to be thinking and praying for me.

The HSI team leader informed the company office. She informed them of my condition and asked for prayers.

Another coworker from Habilitative Services, Carol, talked to our neighbors at the group home Judy and her daughter Katie and told them what happened. Judy was a teacher at the parochial school and had both our daughters, Louise and Rose, in her science class, poor Judy!

Anyway, Carol knew Judy was a retired teacher at the school and she knew us from the group home and school. Carol asked her if there was a prayer group at the Cathedral and to put me on it. Carol said Judy told her she'd do it right now and walked over there with their little dog to do so. Interestingly, the group home and Judy's house just "happened" to be four blocks away from the Cathedral. Don't tell me that's a coincidence too! Carol went the extra mile and sent a card with money to help us out. Now another group of people from Cathedral in New Ulm said prayers for me.

OTHER TYPES OF PRAYERS

Prayers are being heard now, too, from coworkers and office staff. We had at least four staff at the time working for this site. Our team leader also put me on a PTO donation request list for staff to donate time if they could. She knew I didn't have much PTO left and I had also donated PTO in the past for others. Now, eight more people prayed for me as well as more types of prayer added.

Over the years, Rod and I have met co-worker's families. Our HSI's team leader called her mom and dad and sisters to let them know what was going on. Larry probably called his sister, who is in New Ulm to let her know what was going on as well. There were at least ten more people who prayed for me.

MORE FRIENDS— Rod also tried contacting a friend of mine, Ann in West Salem, Wisconsin. She and I met in high school years back actually at a girl scout camp, and became such good friends have always been in touch! One more friend praying for me.

One of the first people Rod called in New Ulm were our neighbors and friends, Curt and Ann. The beauty of this is they have a big family, ten children plus one son-in-law, and we are the godparents to one of their sons! Now, 11 more people prayed for me all from the act of one phone call. They looked after the house while we were away. Their daughter, made me a card when I came home. It's very sweet. She comes over to play with our oldest granddaughter and they love to draw— 10 more people praying for me.

Then Louise, our daughter, contacted our other neighbors, Dave and Nikki. They gladly wanted to help and picked up our mail for us, and also started praying for me. They have five children— one in heaven. They also have brothers and sister in town so told them about my condition and at least six more people prayed for me.

As mentioned, back at home, Louise contacted our church's prayer chain chairperson, and left a message for her to put me on the prayer chain to which I have been a part. Our prayer chain coordinator couldn't quite hear the whole message so she decided to go the extra mile and called Louise to confirm who the prayer request was for because she couldn't believe it was for me.

This is how people help, and do some good; people working with people. People keep trying until they figure out what they need is rather than going with a guess. Louise explained to our prayer coordinator what happened. Louise told her how my heart attack was totally unexpected as I had no prior symptoms and was even at work when it happened. Our chairperson added me on the prayer list right away and others heard through word of mouth. Now, more prayers working for me and another group.

Rod and I volunteer our time for Eucharistic Adoration on Tuesday mornings at 5:00 a.m. Rod called our coordinator to let her know what happened so she can find a sub for me. Our coordinator is surprised, too, that it is me who went in and lets a sister of hers know so she can pray for me.

Between Rod and Louise, they called and Facebooked friends and another church group Together Encounter Christ (TEC) people to have them add me to their prayer chains. This as you can imagine involved many people who also contacted others, they know who have said prayers for me and more clergy. Yet more people said prayers for me all around the state of Minnesota. I can't even guess at the number here of people prayed for me.

Rod called our friend, Phil in Fosston, Minnesota. Phil's been a life-long friend… well, life-long from when we met him in Fosston in the early 1980s. We're his daughter's godparents. Phil has one son, Jonathan, too. Phil contacted Clara from our old church up there, St. Mary's who put us on the church's prayer chain. She was the church's office manager in Fosston for many years. She also weekly added me on the list of petitions said during Mass.

Rod contacted our friends, Lorinda and Jim, on Facebook who are from Fosston. They've been friends since before we've been married over 30 years! Lorinda said actually just the other day (March 10, 2015) that she found out because Rod Facebooked her. Then, she contacted JoAnn and Dale because she knew they were on their way down for vacation.

When Lorinda and her husband, Jim, found out, they contacted their daughter. She's in college at Mankato State. Among all of our Fosston friends over ten more people prayed for me and another church with around 500 parishioners.

Rod continued to call our friends; Russ in Fosston, and Neal and Cindy in Avon, Minnesota. They have one son. and contacted our good friend Terry and his wife, Jody. They, too, have been friends of ours before we were married. Now, six more people prayed for me. You can see now how many more people are connected in prayers for me. One phone call started all this goodness, one call makes all the difference in the world to the point of someone surviving! Yet all this goodness is always left unnoticed!

Rod then texted our good friend, Cindy, who we met in Fosston and is out in North Dakota somewhere. We had visited her via e-mails and she couldn't believe what happened to me either.

Phil also contacted his in-laws, Ann and Francis, who live in Red Lake Falls and prayed for me. They said their hour of Adoration for me and sent a card later. It was so great to hear from them! Between their hour of Adoration for me, along with the petitions I received from the church of St. Mary in Fosston, I realized how many more different *forms* of prayer were said, all on my behalf. Thank you, Ann and Francis and Clara— three more people prayed for me. I wondered, I still don't know what I had done to deserve all these prayers, and how was I ever going to thank everyone!

After I realized all those prayers and goodness were said for me, I realized, more and more how GREAT people are. I knew this all along too, people were great, of course, but when so much negativity is around you from the media, you forget how GREAT people are and all the good that can come out of a situation when people work together. After I heard about all those prayers that were being said for me just started making me realize again that **PEOPLE ARE GREAT AND MAYBE THEY NEED TO HEAR MORE POSITIVE THINGS ABOUT THEIR ACTS OF PRAYER TOO!**

You can see from all those prayers listed how my sister, Nancy's statement was correct that there were hundreds of people who prayed for me, in different states, countries and forms of prayer that made me heal. As a matter of fact, I have a difficult time counting the number of prayers; it seems like the number is infinite because there's no way to count every single prayer.

From this list, at least 15 different states, and one other country said prayers for me. I couldn't believe those totals myself. All this goodness, again, started with one phone call and one prayer. One! A life was spared because of one phone call which led to all these prayers. THANK YOU TO ALL OF YOU AGAIN FOR THOSE PRAYERS! THEY WILL ALWAYS BE REMEMBERED!

www.ingramcontent.com/pod-product-compliance
Lightning Source LLC
Chambersburg PA
CBHW030322100526
44592CB00010B/532
9781950596904